MAPPING

the

CIVIL WAR

Featuring Rare Maps
From the Library of Congress

Dedication

*To my wife, who has always wanted to have a book dedicated to her,
and who fully deserves this one, with my love and thanks. —Christopher Nelson*

Other titles in the Library of Congress Classics Series are:
America's Botanical Beauty
Americans on the Move
The Book in America
Celebration of American Food
The First Americans
Invention in America
The Library of Congress
Prints of the West

Designed by Peggy Robertson
Map influence statements by Michael Wheeler
Copyright © 1992 by Fulcrum Publishing
Printed in China

Library of Congress Cataloging-in-Publication Data

Nelson, Christopher, 1944-
   Mapping the Civil War: featuring rare maps from the Library of Congress / text by Chrisopher Nelson; captions by Brian Pohanka.
Includes bibliographical references and index.
ISBN 1-56373-001-4:
   1. United States—History—Civil War, 1861-1865. 2. United States—History—Civil War, 1861-1865—Maps. I. Pohanka, Brian C., 1955- II. Library of Congress. Geography and Map Division. III. Title.
E468.N38   1992
973.7'022'3—dc20   92-17799
                                                        CIP

Fulcrum Publishing
350 Indiana Street, Suite 350
Golden, Colorado 80401-5093
(800) 992-2908 • (303) 277-1623
www.fulcrum-books.com

MAPPING
the
CIVIL WAR

Featuring Rare Maps
From the Library of Congress

TEXT BY
Christopher Nelson

CAPTIONS BY
Brian Pohanka

FULCRUM PUBLISHING INC.

Jedediah Hotchkiss, renowned Confederate cartographer, used these notebooks for his preliminary sketches. The folded linen map was used by Sherman's field-grade officers; the use of linen allowed for oft-needed rinsing, and easy folding.

CONTENTS

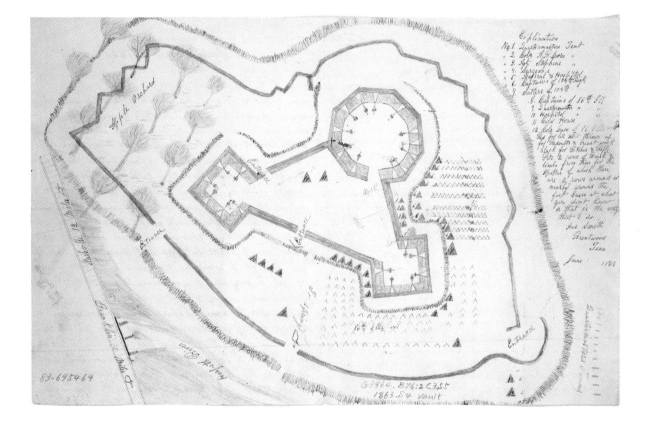

In a letter to a friend, Anson Smith, a Union soldier serving with the 104th Illinois, included this sketch map of a fortification this regiment constructed at Brentwood, Tennessee, in the summer of 1863. The fort was one of a series of earthworks that guarded the strategically vital Louisville and Nashville Railroad.

Editor's Preface

Second in the Library of Congress Classics Series, this book has been an education.

The challenge of bringing the impressive collection of Civil War Maps into a book was exciting; by focusing on contemporary manuscript and printed maps and thereby trying to come close in time to the actual battles, we've tried to bring a freshness to the subject.

After spending many hours selecting maps, I knew I was on the right track when, on presenting the selections to our authors, they said more than once "I've never seen such a beautiful map in my life." Like young boys with a new toy, they couldn't be quiet as we looked through and discussed each map you'll see in the following pages. Their excitement was catching, and it was a losing battle to remind them we were in a library, and should try to be quiet.

Our inclusion here, too, of several Charles Reed sketches, most unpublished until now, helps to bring the subject very close. Many of them were taken from the pages of Reed's letters to his mother and his sweetheart. I chose these pencil and ink sketches for the most part because the quick strokes capture the humanness and the immediacy so much better than do finished, printed drawings.

Of course, no matter how many hours I spent in research, there would be little hope of properly mining the richness of the collection without the help of many people. In addition to our terrific authors, I must thank Dana Pratt, Director of Publishing and Margaret Wagner, Special Projects Coordinator of the Library's Publishing Office—our colleagues in this project. Thanks are due, too, to Bob Morris who lugged more than his fair share of the huge maps I needed to see, and to Ron Grim and all the others in the Geography and Map Division for putting up with my long lists of requests. As always, thanks go to Reid Baker and the photoduplication department for the beautiful photography you see throughout the book. I also give hearty thanks to Dick Stephenson, whose extensive knowledge helped me in choosing the very best maps for this book.

We hope you enjoy this book as much as we've enjoyed bringing it together.

Lynne Shaner
Series Editor
Editorial and Production Director

FORTRESS MONROE, OLD POINT COMFORT AND HYGEIA HOTEL, V.ª

Fortress Monroe, the Federal bastion at the southern tip of the peninsula formed by Virginia's York and James Rivers, was depicted in an 1861 lithograph printed by E. Sachse & Co. of Baltimore, Maryland. The fort provided a secure base for military and naval operations against the Confederate capital, Richmond.

Foreword

*T*he American Civil War lasted only four terrible years, but the nation forevermore was changed economically, politically, and socially. Millions upon millions of words have been written to explain and analyze virtually every facet of this critical period in American history. One aspect that has been largely ignored by most writers, however, is the maps made and used during the Civil War. Although a great wealth of contemporary manuscript and printed maps is extant in archives and libraries throughout the United States, especially at the National Archives and the Library of Congress in Washington, D.C., few authors, editors, or publishers of today's books and articles on the war avail themselves of this valuable resource.[1] Maps and sketches are not seriously examined or studied in relationship to the events of a campaign or battle and are frequently ignored as items suitable to serve as book or journal illustrations. A rare exception is Fulcrum Publishing's *Battle Maps of the Civil War Featuring Rare Maps from the Library of Congress.* In this book, appropriate contemporary manuscript and printed maps have been selected from the collections of the Geography and Map Division and the Manuscript Division of the Library of Congress, and beautifully reproduced in full color to provide the framework for the historical narratives that trace the principal campaigns and battles of the Civil War.

The story of mapping during the Civil War is a fascinating topic worthy of examination. When hostilities erupted in the spring of 1861, there was a critical need for maps by military authorities in the North as well as in the South. Of the few maps that were readily available, many were out of date or sadly lacking the information needed to prosecute the war. The plight of field commanders early in the war is succinctly conveyed by General George B. McClellan's comment that during the 1862 Peninsula Campaign, "correct local maps were not to be found, and the country, though known in its general features, we found to be inaccurately described in essential particulars, in the only maps and geographical memoirs or papers to which access could be had; erroneous courses to streams and roads were frequently given, and no dependence could be placed on the information thus derived."[2]

This lack of knowledge of the geography of the Peninsula, that is the land between the York and James Rivers in Virginia, was shared by Confederate field officers as well. Confederate General Richard Taylor noted that they "knew no more about the topography of the country than they did about Central Africa. Here was a limited district, the whole of it within a day's march of the city of Richmond...and yet we were profoundly ignorant of the country, were without maps, sketches, or proper guides, and nearly as helpless as if we had been suddenly transferred to the banks of the Lualaba (Congo River)."[3]

As a consequence of this lack of accurate maps, both Union and Confederate governments had to devote significant manpower to produce maps suitable for military purposes. Because the North had command of long-established federal mapping units, and printing facilities in which to reproduce them, it was able to quickly produce maps and charts in unprecedented numbers. By 1864 the North's two major map producers, the United States Coast Survey and the Army's Corps of Engineers, were furnishing some 43,000 maps annuallyfor the military — exclusive of the thousands of manuscript maps and sketches prepared by staff in the field and in Washington. In addition, the Coast Survey printed nearly 44,000 nautical charts, with many of them being distributed to the United States naval vessels blockading the Atlantic and Gulf coast harbors and rivers.

The South was not so fortunate. Map production was considerably hampered by the lack of existing agencies and trained personnel, and also by the lack of printing equipment, paper, and ink. Throughout the war, the Confederate Army had difficulty in supplying its field officers with adequate maps. The situation was further complicated by the almost total absence of surveying and drafting equipment, and the lack of trained military engineers and mapmakers to use the equipment that was available.

At the beginning of the war, when requests for maps were received in the Topographical Department of the Army of Northern Virginia, a draftsman was assigned to make a tracing of a pen-and-ink file copy if one existed. This was so time-consuming, however, that Major Albert H. Campbell, in charge of the office, introduced an ingenious "sunprinting" technique as a means of reducing the time required to duplicate maps. According to Campbell, the process involved making copies of maps on tracing paper with India ink, exposing these to sunlight to obtain negatives, and using these negatives to create multiple copies. Although crude in comparison to maps being produced in the North, the sunprints were adequate, and, being timely, were indispensable to officers in the field.

The finest topographical engineer to serve in the Confederate army was a school- master from Staunton, Virginia, named Jedediah Hotchkiss. Born and educated in Windsor, New York, Hotchkiss moved to the Shenandoah Valley where he became the principal of a small rural school called Mossy Creek Academy in 1848. Hotchkiss was not trained to be a topographer or mapmaker, but at an early age he developed strong interests in the related fields of geography and geology. Shortly after joining the staff of General Thomas J. ("Stonewall") Jackson in March 1862, Hotchkiss instructed to "make me a map of the Valley, from Harper's Ferry to Lexington, showing all the points of offence and defence in those places."[4] The resulting comprehensive map, drawn on tracing linen at the scale of 1:80,000 and measuring 254 by 111 cm., was of significant value to Jackson and his staff in planning and executing the Valley Campaign in May and June 1862. Hotchkiss's Valley map is far superior to any manuscript or printed map available to Federal field commanders at anytime during the war.

Conducted against numerically superior forces, the Valley Campaign is considered "one of the most brilliant operations of military history."[5] The success of General Jackson's actions and movements so disturbed Federal planning that large numbers of troops were withheld from McClellan's advance on Richmond. Conceivably, without the aid of superior maps, Jackson's diversionary efforts would not have succeeded and McClellan's movements on Richmond would have had a different ending.

The map of the Shenandoah Valley constructed for Jackson, part of which is reproduced here on the end papers, is part of the Jedediah Hotchkiss map collection in the Geography and Map Division of the Library of Congress. Acquired in 1948, along with Hotchkiss's diaries, correspondence, and private papers, this is one of the finest collections of Confederate maps in existence today. In addition to the Valley map, there are countless sketches, reconnaissance maps, county maps, regional maps, and battle maps. For additional examples of his maps, see pages 49, 58, 64-5, 152, 156, 158.

As the war progressed, field and harbor surveys, topographic and hydrographic surveys, reconnaissances, and road traverses by Federal mappers led to the publication of maps and charts in unprecedented numbers. The development and growing sophistication of the Union mapping effort was apparent in 1864 when it became possible for Coast Survey officials to compile a uniform, ten-mile-to-the-inch base map described by the Survey's Superintendent as "the area of all the States in rebellion east of the Mississippi river, excepting the back districts of North and South Carolina, and the neutral part of Tennessee and to southern Florida, in which no military movements have taken place." Morever, as the Superintendent noted, the map was placed on lithographic stones so that "any limits for a special map may be chosen at pleasure, and a sheet issued promptly when needed in prospective military movements."[6]

When time permitted, topographical engineers in both armies were called upon to prepare accurate, carefully executed maps of fields of battle and fortifications. Many of these maps were used to illustrate official reports of field commanders or were sent back to headquarters in Washington and Richmond for placement in the official files (see pages 35, 44, 49, 109, 136, 138, 140).

Although all successful field commanders realized the necessity of clearly understanding the lay of the land over which they were moving or fighting, some placed a higher value on mapping activities than others. Certainly "Stonewall" Jackson appreciated the value of maps as we have seen by his reliance on the work of his topographical engineer Jedediah Hotchkiss. Another field commander who clearly understood the importance of maps was General William Tecumseh Sherman. Immediately upon assuming command of the Military Division of the Mississippi on March 18, 1864, Sherman began to prepare to meet and defeat the Army of Tennessee and capture the manufacturing and communications center of Atlanta, Georgia. Before beginning operations against the enemy, Colonel William E. Merrill, chief engineer of the Topographical Department, Army of the Cumberland, was ordered to prepare a campaign map.

Merrill's office was well-staffed and equipped for the undertaking. Thomas B. Van Horne in his *History of the Army of the Cumberland* wrote in 1875 that "the army was so far from Washington that it had to have a complete map establishment of its own. Accordingly the office...contained a printing press, two lithographic presses, one photographic establishment, arrangements for map-mounting, and a full corps of draughtsmen and assistants."[7]

The lithographic presses were invaluable for providing multiple copies of a map within a short span of time. The weight of the presses and stones made transporting them difficult, however, requiring that they remain in a central depot near the front lines. When only a few copies of a sketch or road traverse were needed, the Topographical Department would use a process developed by Colonel Merrill's chief assistant, Captain William C. Margedant for photographing the map on paper impregnated with nitrate of silver. The map of the environs of Resaca, Georgia, is an example of a quickly made field map produced by photography. (See page 144)

To begin the campaign map, the Topographical Department obtained a copy of James R. Butts's "Map of the State of Georgia" published in 1859 and enlarged it to the scale of an inch to the mile. According to Van Horne, this was then "elaborated by cross-questioning refugees, spies, prisoners, peddlers, and any and all persons familiar with the country in front of us. It was remarkable how vastly our maps were improved by this process. The best illustration of the value of this method is the fact that Snake Creek Gap, through which our whole army turned, the strong positions at Dalton and Buzzard Roost Gap, was not to be found on any printed map that we could get, and the knowledge of the existence of this gap was of immense importance to us."[8]

Two days before the Atlanta Campaign began, the Topographical Department was informed of the date of advance. Working around the clock, the manuscript map was finished, transferred to four lithographic stones and printed in two hundred copies. For ease of handling, the finished map, which measured 94 x 88 cm. was cut into 24 sections and mounted on cloth to fold to 16 x 23 cm. Van Horne relates that "before the commanding generals left Chattanooga, each had received a bound copy of the map, and before we struck the enemy, every brigade, division, and corps commander in the three armies had a copy."[9]

In addition to the standard edition of the campaign map lithographed on paper, it was also printed directly on muslin and issued in three or possibly four parts. Van Horne points out that this was mainly for the convenience of the cavalry, "as such maps could be washed clean whenever soiled and could not be injured by hard service."[10]

Entitled "Map of Northern Georgia" and dated May 2, 1864, the campaign map served as the principal reference for all field commanders in the initial stages of the campaign. "Although our map became less and less accurate as we advanced south from Chattanooga," Van Horne admitted, "it was still valuable even where its information was defective, because every subordinate commander had the same map as the commanding general, and therefore knew at once from the nature of his orders what he was expected to do. If a road could not be found, still the general direction and the general object of his march could be devined [sic], and the spirit of the general's orders could be faithfully carried out."[11]

That Sherman and his field commanders relied on this map at the beginning of the campaign there can be no doubt. Sherman, for example, ordered General James B. McPherson to fortify his position at Snake Creek Gap in the event that it was necessary to send the bulk of his armies through this passage. (See page 146) "I have sent one of Hooker's divisions to you," he noted. "You should post them in support, with one regiment on the mountain to the east of the gap, not far from the letter 'M' or 'O' in the word 'mountain' east of Villanow. This would prevent the occupation of this mountain, by which the pass would be made dangerous from sharpshooters."[12] Although not explained in the dispatch, it is obvious that Sherman was basing the deployment of these troops on the appearance of the topography and lettering as shown on the campaign map. Furthermore, he clearly expected his field commander to understand this cryptic message. In reply, General McPherson reported in kind: "Brigadier General Williams has reported his division at the west end of the gap, and I have directed him to leave one brigade there to guard the trains and to bring the other two through to this side, posting one regiment on the crest of the mountain near the letter 'M' on the northeast side of the mountain."[13]

The importance that General Sherman attached to the survey work of the topographical engineers in the field and the compilation of new maps from their surveys is revealed in his Special Field Orders no. 15 issued in the field, near Dallas, Georgia, May 31, 1864. The orders read as follows:

In order to secure the rapid and efficient co-working of the topographical engineer department of the army in the field, and to avoid making surveys of any road by more than one officer, the following system will be adopted:

I. No topographical engineer shall be employed as an aide-de-camp or in any other duty than in making purely military surveys. The selection of camps, location of picket-lines, and repairs of roads are not to be imposed on them, but on quartermasters and on other officers.

II. On a march they will survey the route of their commands. When the army comes to a permanent or temporary halt, they will report in person to the chief engineer of their respective departments and make such special field surveys as may be assigned them, at all times complying with his orders and instructions. Their surveys will then be compiled, and maps will be sent to their chiefs, who will cause them to be consolidated and issued from time to time as the exigencies of the campaign will permit.

III. All corps, division, and brigade commanders will assist their topographical engineers to work in harmony and for the benefit on the whole army, and thus secure the data from which to compile, at the earliest possible moment, maps which are indispensably necessary in military movements, as in this manner only can all general officers receive the benefit of all military surveys. By order of Maj. Gen. W. T. Sherman: L. M. Dayton, Aide-de-Camp.[14]

With the recognition of the importance of field surveying and mapping by the commanding general, there can be little doubt that, as Van Horne put it, "the army that General Sherman led to Atlanta was the best supplied with maps of any that fought in the Civil War."[15]

Throughout the Civil War, commercial publishers in the North, and to a lesser extent in the South, produced countless maps to satisfy the general public's interest in up-to-date geographical information. Few families were without someone in the armed forces serving in some little-known place in the South or West. Aware of the great public need for maps, and unhampered by shortages of manpower, paper, ink, and presses, the well-established printing houses in such northern cities as New York, Philadelphia, Boston, and Washington, D.C. began to issue maps in quantities undreamed of before the War. Ralph Waldo Emerson observed in 1865 that "in every house & shop, an American map has been unrolled, & daily studied."[16] Maps of all kinds, such as theater of war maps (page 81), thematic maps (32), pictorial maps, battle maps (75, 96, 160, 169), and panoramic maps or bird's-eye views were printed by lithography, then hand colored, and sold at a reasonable price to citizens at home as well as to officers and enlisted men in the field.

By providing much-needed geographical information, Union and Confederate mapmakers contributed significantly to the operations of the armies in the field. Countless thousands of manuscript, printed and photoprocessed maps were made, many under difficult circumstances, of little-known rural areas in the South and Middle Atlantic States. Little recognition has been paid to the accomplishments and contributions of this small group of men—their maps and sketches are rarely used today to illustrate critical events of the war or to provide insight into the actions of commanders in the field. Perhaps Colonel William Merrill summed it up best when he complained privately that "our daily issue of maps in the field I think deserved a passing mention."[17]

Richard W. Stephenson

References

[1] For reference to maps, see *A Guide to Civil War Maps in the National Archives* (Washington D.C.: The National Archives, 1986) 139pp., and Richard W. Stephenson, *Civil War Maps: An Annotated List of Maps and Atlases in the Library of Congress* (Washington D.C.: Library of Congress, 1989), 410pp.

[2] George B. McClellan, *Report on the Organization and Campaigns of the Army of the Potomac* (New York: Sheldon & Co., 1864), p.157.

[3] Richard Taylor, *Destruction and Reconstruction: Personal Experiences of the Late War*, Richard Harwell, ed. (New York: Longmans, Green & Co., 1955), p.99.

[4] Jedediah Hotchkiss, *Make Me a Map of the Valley: The Civil War Journal of Stonewall Jackso, Topographer,* Archie P. McDonald, ed. foreword by T. Harry Williams (Dallas: Southern Methodis University Press, 1973), p.10.

[5] Mark May Boatner III, *The Civil War Dictionary* (New York: David McKay Co., Inc., 1959), p.739.

[6] U.S. Coast Survey, *Report of the Superintendent of the Coast Survey, Showing the Progress of the Survey During the Year 1864* (Washington D.C.: Government Printing Office, 1866), p.111.

[7] Thomas B. Van Horne, *History of the Army of the Cumberland*, vol. 2 (Cincinnati: Robert Clarke & Co., 1875), p.456.

[8] Ibid., p.457.

[9] Ibid., pp.457-458.

[10] Ibid., p.458.

[11] Ibid.

[12] U.S. War Department, *The War of the Rebellion: A Compilation of the Official Records of the Union and Confederate Armies* (Washington D.C.: Government Printing Office, 1880-1901, series 1, vol. 38, part 4, 1891), p.125.

[13] Ibid., pp.125-126.

[14] Ibid., p.371.

[15] Van Horne, *History of the Army of the Cumberland*, vol. 2, p.358.

[16] Ralph Waldo Emerson, *The Journals and Miscellaneous Notebooks of Ralph Waldo Emerson*, vol. XV, 1860-1866, Linda Allardt, David W. Hill and Ruth G. Bennett, eds. (Cambridge, Mass. and London, England: The Belknap Press of Harvard University Press, 1982), p.64.

[17] William E. Merrill to Orlando M. Poe, October 28, 1864. Orlando M. Poe papers, container 4, general correspondence 1864, Manuscript Division, Library of Congress.

The following list gives the page number of every map in this volume and its corresponding Library of Congress Geography and Map Division number. For example, on page 6, the map is number 396.35.

(6)396.35; (8)547; (17)567.5; (18)678; (20)H110; (23)H86; (24)566.2; (27)12.7; (28-29)564.9; (30)11; (31)34; (32)13.2; (35)416; (42,43)436; (44)417; (49)H90; (57)H96; (58)H97; (64,65)H99; (66)453; (70)673.7; (73)621; (75)252; (78)H109; (79)H112; (81)677; (87)278; (90)281.5; (96)331; (101)327; (102)325; (109)402; (111)159; (112)398.2; (120)657; (126)H168; (128)663; (133)S29; (136)77 [3 maps]; (138)77; (140)77; (143)S39; (144)S102; (146)S101; (152)H187; (156)H185; (158)H10; (160)524; (162)613; (169)607; (171)525.

Chapter 1

First Manassas

*I*t is hard for the modern mind to comprehend the ignorance, the naivete, the innocence with which the amateur armies of 1861 clashed on a boiling July day on the Plains of Manassas. The battle was called First Manassas by the victorious Confederates, and Bull Run by the astonished and disconsolate North.

They wore their best uniforms, Yankees often in gray and Rebels sometimes in blue. They sang going into battle, and small boys beat the drums. Of course they were frightened, but it would have been unthinkable to admit it, for fear of being thought unmanly. In the strain and horror of battle, men learned to recognize fear soon enough, and many broke and ran, oblivious to their honor, their friends, indeed to anything but the panic that drove them from the field.

But that July 21 most didn't run; many were shot or captured, instead of surviving to fight another day. What was perhaps most remarkable was that the men and boys fought as well as they did, and that their leaders made as few mistakes as they did.

The Civil War has been called "the first modern war," and in many ways it was. It saw the first large-scale use of railroads and steam engines to transport and supply armies in the field. Metallic cartridges and breech-loading, multi-shot weapons were used in large numbers. Ironclad warships and submarine mines were introduced, and soldiers first suffered the horrors of extended trench warfare.

The war had even greater impact on the home front, as it hastened the rise of the centralized industrial state required to support it. The South eventually lost because its largely agrarian

This ink and watercolor manuscript map shows the position of Captain Schaeffer's command at First Bull Run, and brings home the knowledge that the height of corn, the depth of the river, and the landmark poplar tree all had some effect on the battle.

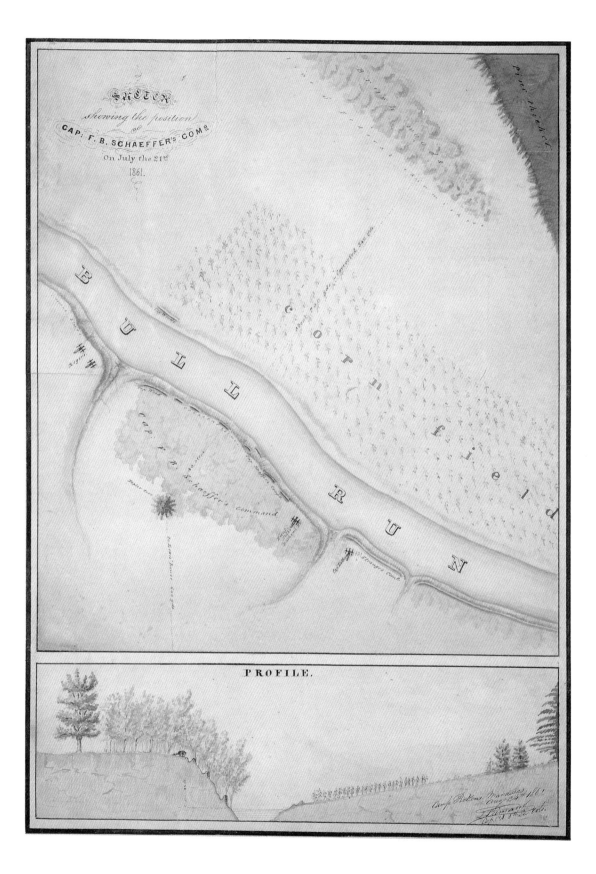

SKETCH

showing the position
of
CAP. F. B. SCHAEFFER'S COM.ᴰ
On July the 21.ˢᵗ
1861.

BULL RUN

Cornfield

Cap. F. B. Schaeffer's Command

PROFILE.

17

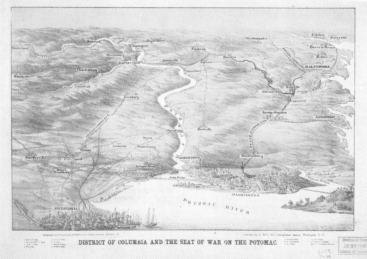

DISTRICT OF COLUMBIA AND THE SEAT OF WAR ON THE POTOMAC.

While stylized, this Olympian-eye view of Washington, D.C. and vicinity graphically depicts the water, road and rail approaches to the Federal capital. By the end of May, 1861, Union troops had crossed the Potomac River and occupied Arlington Heights and the town of Alexandria, visible at lower left.

economy couldn't expand enough to face both the North's industry and its invading armies. On each side electric telegraph-aided modern news reporting and a free press had a huge impact on popular politics and the ability of democratic governments to conduct the war.

But the Civil War was also the last of the Napoleonic wars. Men were organized in solid units from the regimental level up to the army, and they fought shoulder to shoulder behind their flags in tactics basically unchanged from Waterloo. Despite the increased range of rifled muskets and artillery, battles often were close-range slugging matches between massed soldiers who could clearly see each other.

The war was also old-fashioned in that most men came to it with romantic assumptions of chivalry and bravery, and ideas on rules of war and honor, even the sanctity of private property unlucky enough to get in the way. Men felt it was impure to feel fear, and saw defeat as proof that God had withdrawn grace from sinners.

It was a devout age, and each side was convinced of God's sanction. This made casualties even more of a spiritual burden, as soldiers saw that death took men indiscriminately. For civilians, the horror was deepened by the recruiting policies of the day, which urged all of the young men in a small town to join the same company or regiment. One bad day in battle could cripple the future of a whole county. And for a finally defeated South, the post-war mythology of honor and chivalry tried to replace the losses of the battlefield and the reality of total war against civilians and property.

But at First Manassas these lessons were far away. The relatively few professionals on both sides didn't want to fight the battle; at least, they didn't want to fight it yet. They doubted that the civilian volunteers had either the training or discipline to respond to commands which in truth, they knew they were barely qualified to give.

Many of the West Pointers were veterans of the Mexican War, but that triumph of 1848 was won with an army far smaller than the Union forces that approached Bull Run. No field officer in 1861 had ever commanded more than a regiment in battle. Now there were thousands of eager amateurs looking to them for certainty and victory in what everyone at home thought would be the only battle of the war.

But the politicians, the newspaper generals, and the women who had given up their sons and brothers, their husbands and uncles to the huge new armies of democracy didn't, probably couldn't see what the professionals were so worried about. So it was "On to Richmond!," and "On to Washington!", and after stalling as long

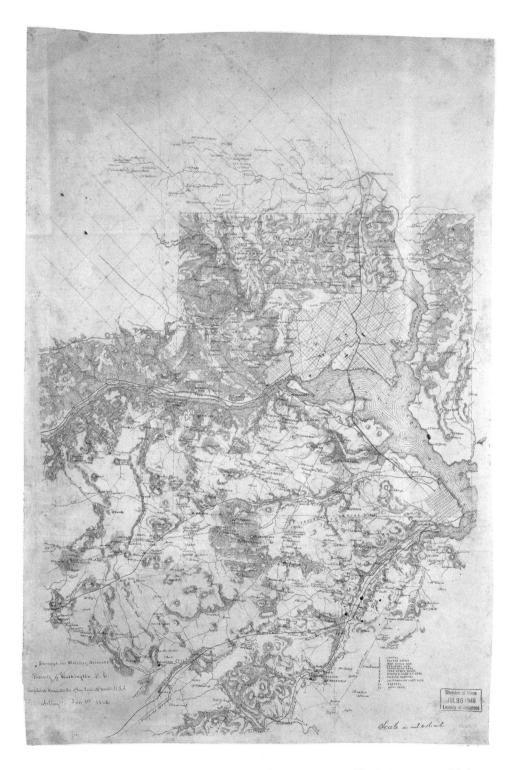

In the wake of its defeat at Bull Run, General Irvin McDowell's Union army withdrew to the safety of the interconnected series of earthen fortifications, batteries and rifle pits that ringed the Federal capitol. This detailed overview of the Washington defenses was published at McDowell's order on New Year's Day, 1862.

Clad in the gray uniforms typical
of pre-war American militiamen, a
squad from the 7th New York gather
at their camp near Washington, D.C.
The elite Manhattan unit was
one of the first to rally to the defense
of the Northern capital.
LC B8151-935

as they could, the generals on both sides started to move.

Objectively, the initial advantages belonged to the Confederates under their joint commanders, Pierre Gustave Toutant Beauregard, the hero of Fort Sumter, and Joseph E. Johnston, a fellow West Pointer and respected colonel in the prewar army. Both were also

Shortly before leading the Federal advance on Manassas, General Irvin McDowell (center), stands with his staff at Arlington — the former home of Robert E. Lee. In the course of the war three of these officers would give their lives : Henry Kingsbury (4th from right), Amiel Whipple (7th from right) and Haldimand Putnam (8th from right).
LC B8184-4099

engineers and Mexican War veterans. Each commanded his own "army," Beauregard the main body of 20,000 and Johnston some 12,000 troops in the Shenandoah Valley.

Beauregard was posted to the Manassas area weeks before the battle, enabling him and his staff to extensively reconnoiter the ground and make badly needed maps of the region. Johnston's job was to safeguard what was to become the "breadbasket" of the Confederacy, a vital natural resource which was to be bitterly contested.

The two Confederate armies were linked by rail, a factor that proved to be critical when the Union's Robert Patterson, a veteran of the War of 1812, failed to keep Johnston pinned down; in the end, the railroads got Johnston's soldiers to Manassas in time to turn the tide of battle.

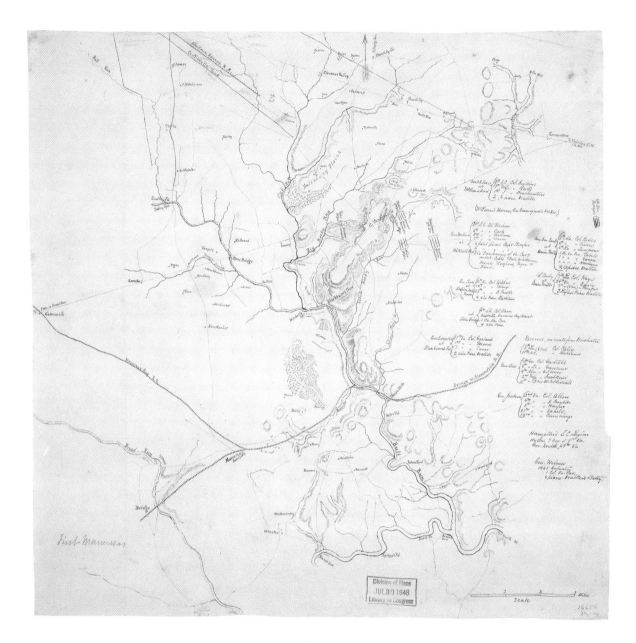

Arrayed against the Confederates was a growing collection of Union volunteers from across the North under Major General Irvin McDowell. A West Pointer, McDowell had Mexican War experience and was capable. McDowell was better known for his gargantuan appetite than for the experience and military distinction that President Lincoln probably sought for the position.

As the three-month enlistments of many Northern militia volunteers were about to expire, McDowell began what became the First Manassas Campaign in early July with a ponderous march from Washington, D.C. He reached Centreville, Virginia by July 18, and

This manuscript map by Jedediah Hotchkiss details the Confederate viewpoint of the battle.

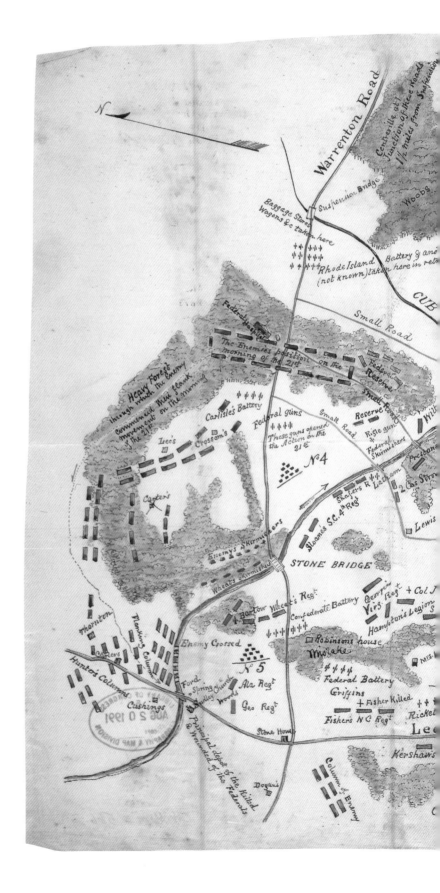

This hand-wrought copy of a lithograph based on sketches made by Captain Samuel P. Mitchell of the 1st Virginia Regiment details troop movements and incidents of the battle of Bull Run, including the locations where prominent Confederate officers fell. This map was hand drawn on linen, and hand colored.

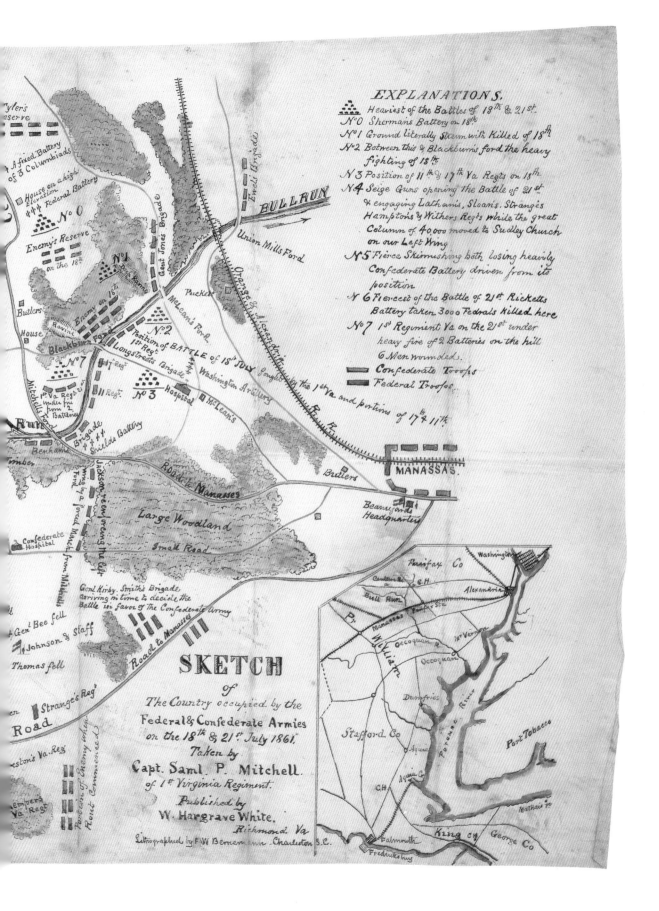

EXPLANATIONS.

Heaviest of the Battles of 18th & 21st.

Nº 0 Shermans Battery on 18th

Nº 1 Ground literally strewn with Killed of 18th

Nº 2 Between this & Blackburns ford the heavy fighting of 18th

N 3 Position of 11th & 17th Va Regts on 18th

N 4 Seige Guns opening the Battle of 21st & engaging Lathams, Sloans. Stranges Hamptons & Withers Regts while the great Column of 40,000 moved to Sudley Church on our Left Wing

Nº 5 Fierce Skirmishing both losing heavily Confederate Battery driven from its position

N 6 Fiercest of the Battle of 21st Ricketts Battery taken 3000 Federals Killed here

Nº 7 1st Regiment Va on the 21st under heavy fire of 2 Batteries on the hill 6 Men wounded.

▬ Confederate Troops
▬ Federal Troops

BULL RUN

MANASSAS.

Beauregards Headquarters

SKETCH

of

The Country occupied by the Federal & Confederate Armies on the 18th & 21st July 1861.

Taken by

Capt. Saml. P. Mitchell

of 1st Virginia Regiment.

Published by

W. Hargrave White.

Richmond Va

Lithographed by F W Bornemann. Charleston S.C.

if the inexperienced Federal supply officers had been able to keep up, McDowell could have overwhelmed Beauregard's 20,000 Rebels. Instead, a reconnaissance in force was ordered over Blackburn's Ford, or Bull Run.

By then, the Confederates had had weeks to scout and map the country and its sketchy road system. This meant that Beauregard and his commanders knew where McDowell's men would have to go and how to maneuver to meet them. McDowell, by contrast, made what is today a twenty-minute car ride from the nation's capital using maps with very little specific detail. This nearly blind leap into the unknown was to be typical of many Civil War campaigns during early years of the war.

In any event, Confederates under commanders including James Longstreet easily threw back the Blackburn's Ford probe. The relatively bloodless fight gave Johnston time to start his men from the Valley to reinforce Beauregard using the railroad to Manassas Junction. Now each army knew that the other was near. Both sides began to plan in earnest for what they considered the decisive battle of the war.

While Beauregard was urging Johnston to join him, McDowell was planning to outflank Beauregard. On the night of the 20th, McDowell spread a large area map out on the floor of his quarters, and gave his assignments: two diversionary Union attacks to mask the main thrust across the Sudley Springs Ford. The diversions would be General Robert Tyler's thrust across a soon-to-be-famous stone bridge over Bull Run, and Colonel Israel Richardson's attack at Blackburn's Ford.

In essence, McDowell planned a massive and daring dash around the Confederate left flank. Ironically, Beauregard also planned an attack around the Union's left, with the result that the two armies pushed each other in a giant circle as the battle developed. But initially, and almost throughout the day, the Union plans were better executed, and the Confederates were confused, and kept on the defensive.

Contributing to the Rebels' problems were muddled orders and inadequate staff work; contributing to the Yankees' ultimate failure was an initially slow execution of the plans which enabled the Confederates to recover from their surprise and their mistakes and rush reinforcements to where they were needed most. The problems experienced by each side in this battle became tendencies that hampered each throughout the war: too few staff to properly carry orders and intelligence for the South, and good plans but slow movement by the North.

Federal reinforcements, led by such commanders as Colonel

Illustrations of colorful early war volunteers and portraits of prominent Federal commanders highlight an 1861 map of the "Western Border States." Despite the pro-Union sympathies of many residents of Missouri, Kentucky and eastern Tennessee, the North faced a long and bloody struggle to occupy and maintain control of the region.

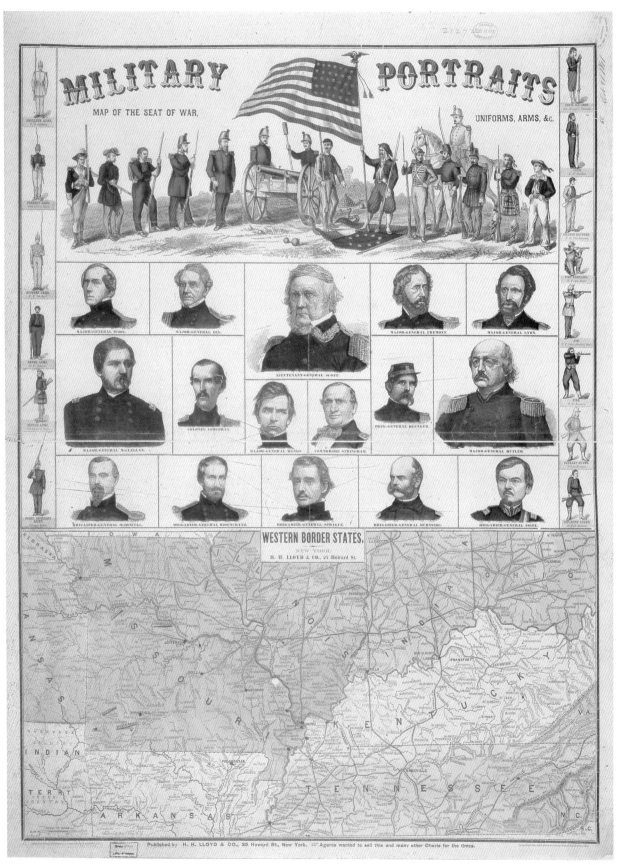

MILITARY PORTRAITS

MAP OF THE SEAT OF WAR,

UNIFORMS, ARMS, &c.

MAJOR-GENERAL WOOL.

MAJOR-GENERAL DIX.

LIEUTENANT-GENERAL SCOTT.

MAJOR-GENERAL FREMONT.

MAJOR-GENERAL LYON.

MAJOR-GENERAL McCLELLAN.

COLONEL CORCORAN.

MAJOR-GENERAL BANKS.

COMMODORE STRINGHAM.

BRIG.-GENERAL BLENKER.

MAJOR-GENERAL BUTLER.

BRIGADIER-GENERAL McDOWELL.

BRIGADIER-GENERAL ROSENCRANZ.

BRIGADIER-GENERAL SPRAGUE.

BRIGADIER-GENERAL BURNSIDE.

BRIGADIER-GENERAL SIGEL.

WESTERN BORDER STATES,
NEW YORK:
H. H. LLOYD & CO., 25 Howard St.

Published by H. H. LLOYD & CO., 25 Howard St., New York. Agents wanted to sell this and many other Charts for the times.

William T. Sherman, joined with General Samuel Heintzelman's main flanking column to drive the Confederates down the hill and across the Warrenton Pike for what the triumphant Unionists hoped would be a final stand on Henry House Hill. If the Confederates could be driven from this dominant geographical feature of the low, rolling fields of Manassas, there was no nearby high ground to fall back to, and the war would be over.

At First Manassas luck or destiny, perhaps, placed an obscure and cranky former mathematics professor from Virginia Military Institute, Thomas Jonathan Jackson, on top of the Widow Henry's hill just as Bee's and Bartow's men came streaming up from Matthew's Hill.

Jackson, a thirty-seven-year-old West Pointer who had seen extensive combat in the Mexican War, carefully placed his brigade behind the plateau's sloping flank and waited. General Bee, desperately trying to reform the fleeing soldiers cried out "There stands Jackson like a stone wall; rally behind the Virginians!" Along the crest of Henry House Hill a line was established from the Manassas Road to the Robinson House, and for the next hour the two armies experienced the grinding horror of 19th-century close order combat.

At first, it looked as if the Union attacks would succeed; Bartow was killed, and Bee mortally wounded; hundreds of others were down; the Widow Henry became the war's first civilian casualty, killed in her bed by a Union artillery shell.

But McDowell made a critical tactical error: he ordered two Federal artillery batteries up the hill without enough infantry support. The batteries established a firing position and had begun to make Jackson's line with enfilading fire when Confederates wearing blue coats charged out of the woods. The confused Yanks held their fire, then fled as the Confederates poured a devastating volley into them and captured the position. Hand-to-hand fighting won and lost the guns three times; finally, the South carried the position and with it the battle.

McDowell couldn't believe that he had been defeated, but his exhausted troops had been marching and fighting for fourteen hours in the heat, and they had nothing left. The Federals started to fall back without orders, and Confederate attacks pushed them faster, as disorganization spread. But it was a grudging pullback, not a rout, until luck struck again in the form of a Rebel artillery shell that exploded in the midst of Union troops on Cub Run Bridge over the Warrenton Pike.

The retreat escalated into a panic of the hundreds of civilians, journalists, politicians, and thrill-seekers who had come out from Washington to enjoy the spectacle. A mixed mass of amateur soldiers

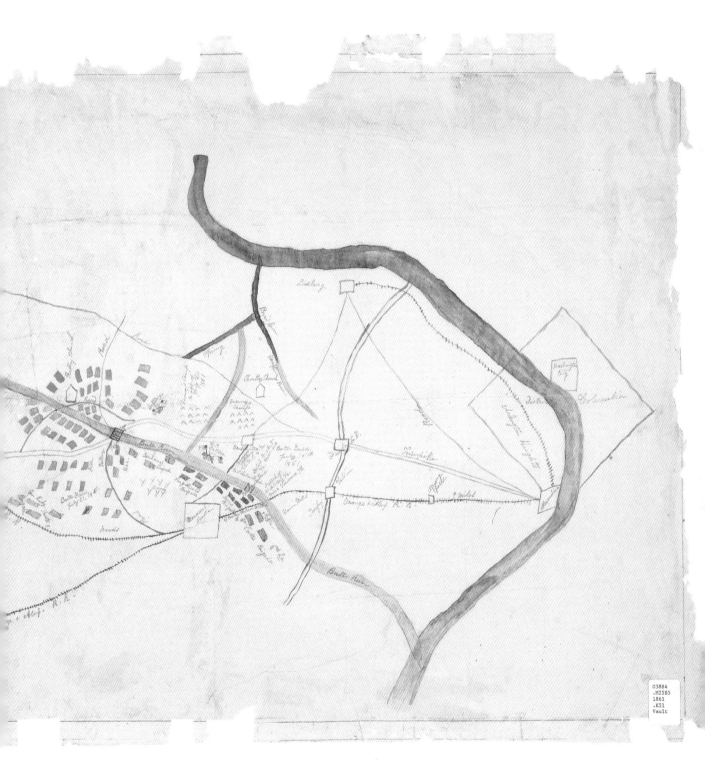

Confederate Captain Porter King, a lawyer who commanded a company in the 4th Alabama Infantry, sketched this overview of the battle of Manassas, the Civil War's first great clash of arms. Bull Run, the stream by which the battle was known in the North, bisects the disputed terrain some 20 miles southwest of Washington, D.C.

A humorous 1861 cartoon published by J.B. Elliot of Cincinnati, Ohio, graphically illustrates the "Anaconda Plan" put forth by Army General-in-Chief Winfield Scott. Scott's strategy was based upon a gradual but inevitable "strangulation" of Confederate resources by means of a naval blockade of Southern ports, and an offensive down the Mississippi River.

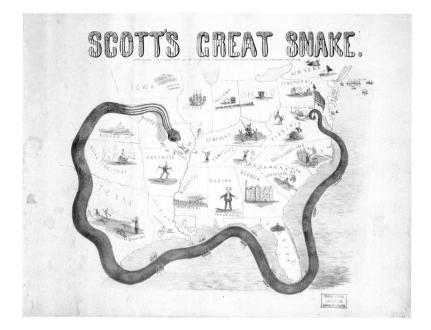

and frightened civilians spent the night trudging back through Centreville and Fairfax and toward Potomac River bridges, and safety.

Confederate morale was still high, but the Southerners were just as exhausted by the heat and fighting as the now-fleeing Yanks. Some, including the newly anointed "Stonewall" Jackson pushed Beauregard to keep up the pursuit, and end the war. But each side was played out. The battle was over.

When we now compare with the huge battles later in the war, First Manassas, or First Bull Run, it does not appear to be an over costly engagement. But as the first great fight of the war its devastation seemed incalculable to both sides: of the 28,452 Union troops actually fighting, 418 were killed, 1,011 were wounded, and 1,214 were missing or captured. Of the combined Confederate armies' 32,232 engaged, 387 were killed, 1,582 were wounded, but only 12 were reported missing or captured.

The biggest casualties at First Manassas, however, were the hopes and illusions of the people North and South; each section thought the other wouldn't really fight, and that the price of victory would be cheap. By the end of the day on July 21, 1861, these illusions and many lives were shattered and no one could see the final outcome.

In 1861, the two main factors that determined what areas were well mapped were population and commerce. The area of probable combat in Northern Virginia, around Centreville and Manassas, was well traveled, and fairly well

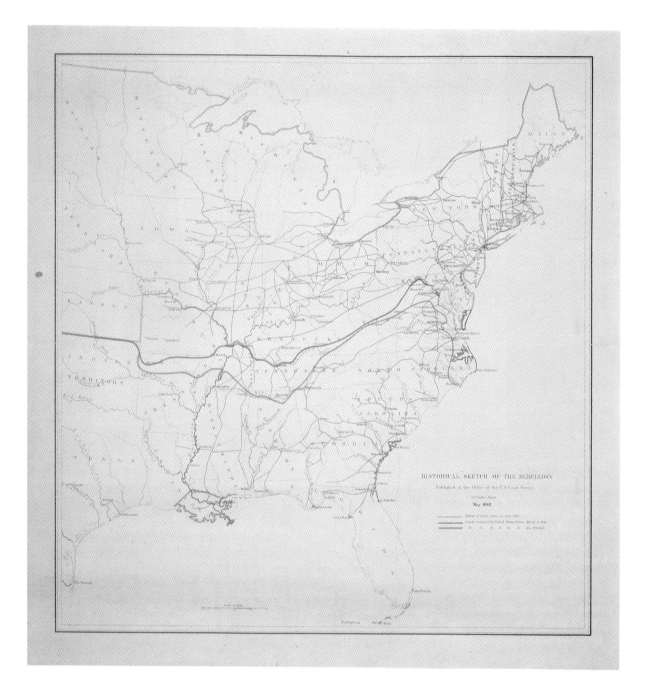

Historical Sketch of the Rebellion

Published at the Office of the U.S. Coast Survey

May 1862

mapped. The Confederates had the advantage of occupying the probable field of battle, so their need for new maps was less critical than the Union's need.

For the Union troops, the information they most needed concerned the crossings of Bull Run. After the Battle of Blackburn's Ford on July 18th, the Northern engineers attempted to probe the stream to determine where it was fordable. The depth of the water and high banks made the stream difficult to cross, as evidenced by Captain Schaeffer's map on page 17. Although these attempts were repulsed by the Confederates, General McDowell got the information he sought from his map. According to his Chief Engineer, Major J.G. Barnard:

The railroad and river transportation network, so crucial to the deployment of Civil War armies and their material, are prominent features of this 1862 map published by the U.S. Coast Survey, which also traces the progressive "limits occupied by United States forces."

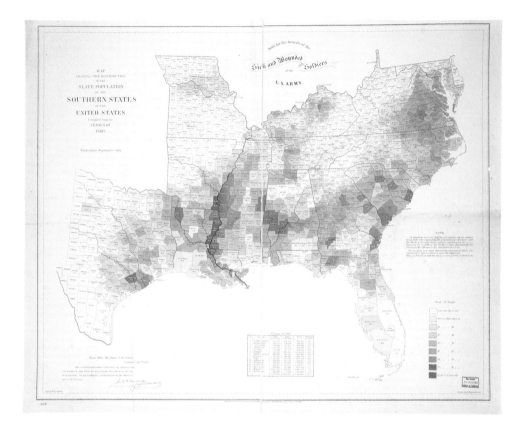

The 1860 Census provided the statistical basis for a county by county profile of the South's slave population. The darker colored counties on the map were those containing the highest percentage of slaves — clear indication that while slavery may have been the primary cause for the American Civil War, most Southerners were not in fact slave-owners.

"Two or three miles above the Warrenton [Stone] Bridge is a ford, laid down on our maps as 'Sudley Spring.'" Reliable information justified the belief that the ford was good; that it was unfortified; that it was watched by only one or two companies...."

The critical military consideration during the battle was the time required for the Union troops to get over the stream and attack the Confederate left flank. As another engineering officer, Captain Woodbury, reported:

"The distance between these points by our route is between five and six miles. We followed in the main an old road as laid down upon the map."

Captain Woodbury later blamed the precious hours lost by the green, undisciplined troops in reaching the ford and crossing the stream for the Union defeat.

It is not clear that the Confederates were aware the road existed. General Beauregard, in his official report, stated:

"The enemy, beginning his detour from the turnpike at a point half-way between stone bridge and Centreville, had pursued a tortuous, narrow trace of a rarely-used road through a dense wood the greater part of his way until near the Sudley Road."

The Confederates responded to the enfilade maneuver with their stand on Henry House Hill, seen on Captain Mitchell's map (pp. 24-25), and by rushing General Kirby Smith's brigade up from the critical railroad junction, seen on Hotchkiss's map (p.23). Most participants in the battle only saw a small portion of the action, and so limited sketches, such as Captain King's, were the norm.

Chapter 2

Fort Henry to Shiloh

*I*t hardly seems possible that a scruffy little man named Hiram Grant could have become the avenging angel of the North who organized the final defeat of the Confederacy. But a congressman's error in signing his appointment to West Point helped create the aptness of the name of the South's nemesis; Grant found that he was listed as "U.S." Grant, so thereafter he was Ulysses Simpson Grant, "Ulys" to his wife, and "Sam" to his friends.

And in the late winter of 1862, at a place called Fort Donelson, the world found out that "U.S." also stood for something more ominous for the Confederacy: Unconditional Surrender.

Grant, like Lincoln, was a midwesterner, and he shared the view of his region's business and political elites that whatever might be happening back East, the Confederates' closing of the Mississippi, the Cumberland, and other vital economic river highways had to be reversed. The Mississippi and its tributaries formed natural "interstate highways" for the producers and traders of North and South alike.

From this perspective, the strategic impetus to Grant's entire career in the Western Theater of the Civil War seems inevitable: Forts Henry and Donelson, followed by bloody Shiloh, were all key river-based campaigns designed to clear the Confederate armies from political and commercial areas vital to the Upper Midwest. These campaigns were the Western armies' contribution to Winfield Scott's original "Anaconda Plan" to surround and slowly strangle the South by land and blockade at sea.

Success at the two forts freed Grant and the Union high command to focus their resources on splitting the Confederacy by opening the Mississippi and linking the Midwest with the markets and resources

Confederate cavalry leader Nathan Bedford Forrest was an untutored military genius whose forceful personality and mastery of strategy and tactics made him one of the most feared and respected Rebel commanders in the war's Western theater.
LC B8171-2908

of the world through the Port of New Orleans, captured shortly after Shiloh.

But if it all seems inevitable and understandable now, at the time it was a near run thing: the South came within an eyelash of checking Grant at Fort Donelson and defeating him at Shiloh. To the war's long list of critical "what if's" must be added the possibility of some other Federal commander succeeding in the Vicksburg Campaign, had Grant failed his opening tests at those river landings in Tennessee.

Following his initial success at the minor Battle of Belmont, in 1861, Grant found himself as but one of six "Illinois" brigadier generals vying for the favor of both President Lincoln and area commander Henry Halleck.

By late 1861, Grant's troops had formed the forward thrust of the Union at Paducah, Kentucky, across from Illinois, while the Episcopal bishop-turned-General Leonidas Polk held the strategic Confederate strongpoint of Columbus, slightly to the southwest. Halleck and other armchair strategists perceived that if Columbus could be flanked, preferably without a fight, then the main body of Confederate forces under General Albert Sidney Johnston further south would eventually be threatened. Looking at the map showed both Halleck and Lincoln that the key to turning Columbus lay at two otherwise obscure river fortifications, Fort Henry, on the Tennessee, and Fort Donelson, on the Cumberland.

Grant had been thinking about the practical aspects of attacking these bastions, and had worked out a cooperative relationship with U.S. Navy flag officer, Andrew Hull Foote. Foote had pulled together an imaginative collection of armored river boats and gunships that proved to be ideally suited to the riverine warfare that so characterized the Civil War.

Grant's small army of 15,000, supported by Foote's seven gunboats, arrived off Fort Henry on February 6, 1862, to the consternation of Confederates who felt secure that the Yankees wouldn't attack in the dead of winter. Fort Henry itself was an unfinished, flooded fieldwork mounting seventeen guns. When Foote's gunboats arrived, the fort's commander, General Lloyd Tilghman, sent most of his 100 gunners down the road to nearby Fort Donelson. After a spirited bombardment from Foote, Tilghman surrendered before Grant's infantry was anywhere in sight, but not before the fort's inexperienced gunners managed to cause considerable damage to the Navy.

General Tilghman, later killed during the Vicksburg campaign, received an "unconditional surrender" demand from Foote, not Grant, and promptly complied. Buoyed by this easy success, and wary that Halleck would call a halt to think things over, Grant immediately marched on Fort Donelson, across the isthmus on the Cumberland River. But the attack on the fort wasn't that easy.

Foote's gunboats had suffered badly in their fight at Fort Henry, and Grant was having trouble persuading his colleague to move quickly, without taking time to refit. In the meantime Albert Sidney Johnston, a man seen by many Southerners as their most able commander, wanted Donelson held long enough to allow a strategic redeployment. If Johnston had not been killed later that year at Shiloh his reputation might have suffered, as many critics saw his moves during this encounter with Grant as an unnecessary retreat right out of Kentucky, causing the abandonment of Nashville, Tennessee by Confederate troops.

While not drawn to scale, this map of Forts Henry and Donelson was intended to note the position and caliber of the artillery deployed in the Confederate earthworks attacked by Union land and naval forces in February, 1862. The plan accompanied a letter written by General George W. Cullum, an engineer officer who served as General Henry Halleck's Chief of Staff.

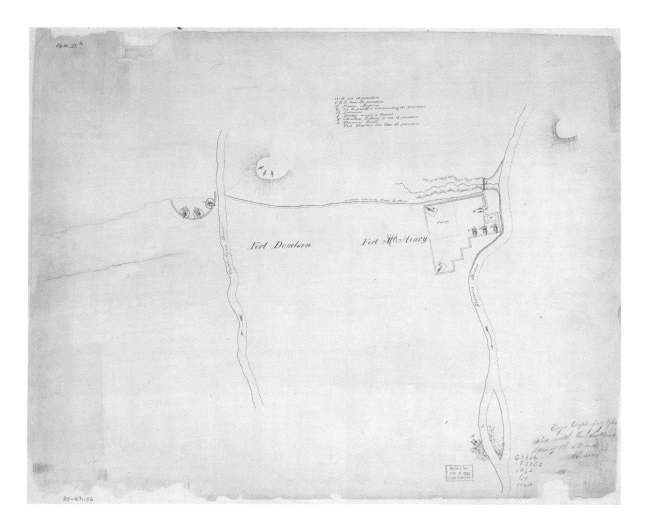

Brandishing a flaming oil torch, a Union signalman relays a nighttime message to a neighboring signal station in this illustration by Alfred Waud. An officer seated atop the signal platform (left) peers through his telescope to observe the reply.
LC USZ62-155

A lithograph from a painting by Confederate soldier-artist Conrad Wise Chapman shows troops of the 3rd Kentucky in their camp at Corinth, Mississippi in May, 1862. A month earlier the regiment had lost 174 men in the battle of Shiloh.

Johnston also had a major problem shared by Grant, of divided commands and the conflicting egos of politicians turned generals. Ultimately, Grant's victory turned on the South's quarrelsome command at Donelson. When Grant's troops arrived after their one-day march from Fort Henry on the 12th, the Confederacy's Gideon J. Pillow and John B. Floyd—a former U.S. Secretary of War—were more or less in command over fellow generals Bushrod Johnson, Simon Bolivar Buckner, and 21,000 men. Adding spice to the leadership stew was then-Colonel Nathan Bedford Forrest, a cavalry commander who had yet to earn the nickname "That Devil Forrest" from his terrified Union opponents.

Floyd, in fairness, had a different interpretation of his orders than did the number two, Pillow, who correctly wanted to hold on to allow the Confederates' retreat from Columbus, Bowling Green, and Nashville, as their orders directed. Floyd, and Buckner wanted to cut their way out while escape was still possible. Johnson supported the group decision to buy time by attacking Grant's infantry, but apparently none of the generals gave any thought to what might happen after their attack. Ironically, the effort was highly successful, and the entire garrison could have easily escaped had Pillow not ordered them back into the fort to face a siege.

Luck was with Grant that February 15th; Pillow had already ordered his withdrawal into the fort when Grant reached the field. This allowed Grant to reorganize his troops and launch counter-assaults that sealed in the now furious Confederate troops, who were beginning to realize the full extent of their leader's failure.

That night, a disgusted Forrest led his 800 men across an icy creek to safety, while Floyd and Pillow found reasons to justify escape. Command devolved to Buckner, ironically an "Old Army" friend of Grant's who, when Grant was down and out, had offered him financial assistance. The next day, Grant accepted the "unconditional surrender" of Fort Donelson, and a disputed number of soldiers, estimated at between 8,000 and 15,000.

So the legend of "Unconditional Surrender Grant" was born, an event of significance that finally outstripped the immediate effects of his capture of the river forts, and the Confederates' panicky abandonment of Kentucky and most of Tennessee. It was Albert Sidney Johnston's belated attempt to repair this damage that led to Grant's next test, Shiloh.

A sketch by Charles W. Reed, entitled "Spooning."

Shiloh

The bloodiest battle of the Civil War to date came at a Tennessee River mud hole called Pittsburgh Landing; indeed, the South often called the battle by that name. But the North, and history, came to call this terrible carnage in April, 1862 "Shiloh," in Hebrew "Place of Peace," after a nearby one-room log Methodist church.

Shiloh was the culmination of Albert Sidney Johnston's determination to regain the strategic initiative the South had lost by its precipitous withdrawal from Kentucky and most of Tennessee, following Grant's victories at Forts Henry and Donelson upriver. Grant, in fact, was using the Pittsburgh Landing area as a handy staging point for a big Federal push on Corinth, Mississippi, the major Confederate stronghold some fifty miles south.

Grant's superior, Henry Halleck, perhaps jealous of the growing adulation for Grant in the North, concocted a silly paper feud after Donelson, and actually removed Grant from command. But shortly before the clash at Shiloh Grant regained control of the forces in the field, to await a junction with Major General Don Carlos Buell's larger, 55,000-man force approaching from eastern Tennessee.

Buell's army had been consolidating Federal control of Nashville, abandoned in the Confederate retreat following Henry and Donelson. What a union of Grant and Buell's armies would mean for the South was apparent to the Confederate high command, and Johnston moved quickly to strike at Pittsburgh Landing while his 40,000 men still outnumbered Grant's force.

Johnston's reorganized command was called the Army of the Mississippi, and his second in command newly arrived from the East was none other than Pierre Beauregard, the victor of Fort Sumter and First Manassas. Their subordinates were scarcely less distinguished, and included as Corps commanders Bishop Leonidas Polk, and the former Vice President of the United States, John C. Breckenridge, of Kentucky. The remaining two corps were under William J. Hardee, the former Commandant of Cadets at West Point and author of an army tactics manual in the knapsack of nearly every officer on both sides, and the disputatious Braxton Bragg, a personal favorite of President Jefferson Davis.

Perhaps because of his subordinate's reputation as a skillful engineer, Johnston let Beauregard draw up the tactical plans for the battle. Johnston focused his energies on getting his force to move rapidly in time to strike Grant on April 4. Shiloh came after a full year of war, but the Western armies of both sides were scarcely better trained and disciplined than the Eastern armies had been at Bull Run, and many of the officers and men suffered from the same misconceptions about the character of the enemy, and what it would take to win the war.

In any event, delays cost the Army of the Mississippi a full day, during which Johnston was certain that his force had been discovered by Grant. In fact, Grant's victories and the precipitous Confederate retreats engendered in both Grant and his second-in-command, Bull Run veteran William T. Sherman, the belief that the South was incapable of offensive action at this point. Neither Grant nor Sherman ordered cavalry patrols that would certainly have discovered Johnston's intentions, nor did they have their outposts dig in. In 1862 both sides still clung to the notion that trenches were unmanly, and robbed an army of the will to advance.

For almost two days Johnston's army camped within earshot of Union regimental commanders whose increasingly startled reports were sarcastically brushed aside by Sherman. On April 6 Grant himself was so unconcerned about a possible Rebel offensive that he was upriver having breakfast when Hardee's men rudely shattered the breakfasts, and delusions, of his unprepared troops.

At first the Confederates succeeded despite the faulty tactical dispositions so carefully arranged by Beauregard. Ignoring the inexperience of the bulk of the army, he had arranged to attack in three massive waves, each a full Corps across, with Breckenridge in reserve. As the waves broke over the Union lines they became a mixed mass of units whose commanders didn't know each other, and whose rushes couldn't be properly coordinated, because the lines of command went sideways, away from the focus of the action.

This critical flaw was not apparent during the first two or three hours of the assault, as the twin forces of surprise and numbers drove back the divisions of Sherman and a brave amateur, Benjamin Prentiss. The small creeks that Sherman had hoped would defend his flank became traps forcing the fleeing Federals into tighter and tighter pockets.

The Confederates' disorganization began to take its toll, however. Recognizing the difficulties, Johnston assigned Corps commanders to sectors, right, left, center. Reflecting their inexperience in managing large units, the generals increasingly wasted their efforts in staff work, personally leading brigades and even regiments "to the sound of the guns," rather than coordinating mass attacks that would have completed the Yankees' rout.

These delays and wasted opportunities gave Union commands under W.H.L. Wallace and Grant's political rival, John A. McClernand, time to rally a line that Prentiss, an Illinois attorney and Mexican War veteran, was to turn into one of the war's legendary actions: The Hornet's Nest. During this rally Grant arrived to encourage Prentiss to hold at all costs, while Grant concentrated on forming an impregnable Union stronghold by the river.

Grant knew precisely what Johnston feared: that if Grant could hold until the arrival of Buell's army, the initiative would go to the Union. For nearly four hours, Prentiss and the remnants of the other Union divisions withstood twelve Confederate assaults. Of the 4,000 Union troops manning the Hornet's Nest, fully 2,000 were shot down, and in the end all were captured.

But it had worked beyond anything Grant or Prentiss had imagined, for in the early afternoon Johnston was mortally wounded leading a charge by one of Breckenridge's brigades. Beauregard took command and as his increasingly exhausted army pushed the Yankees into what appeared to be the final stand by the river, solid ranks of Blue infantry, backed by massed artillery and two navy gunboats, brought the Confederates to a halt.

To the bitter astonishment of Braxton Bragg, whose abilities were only outstripped by his temper, Beauregard declared that the day's victory was "sufficiently complete." The Hero of Fort Sumter had been incorrectly informed that Buell's army hadn't arrived, and that the Confederates could finish their work in the morning. Beauregard triumphantly wired President Davis in Richmond "A Complete Victory."

Bragg and the advance elements of Johnston's army stared down the confused mass of panic-stricken Union soldiers who had fled their units all day, many throwing themselves into the Tennessee, but the Confederates didn't realize that Buell's army was even then disembarking. In fact, Grant's and Sherman's efforts to rally a solid defensive line had been successful, and Grant was planning to renew the offensive when Buell's men started to arrive. Bragg was too late, and Beauregard had missed his great opportunity.

That night Sherman, wounded in the hand but renewed in confidence lost in a nervous collapse months previously, dropped by Grant's headquarters under a tree to share a cigar in the rain, and, he thought, to discuss a prudent retreat. "We've had the devils' own

Louisiana-born Confederate General Pierre Gustave Toutant Beauregard assumed command of the Southern forces after Johnston's mortal wound. Though victorious at Fort Sumter and First Manassas, heavy losses compelled Beauregard to yield the battlefield of Shiloh to his Northern foes.
LC B8184-1685

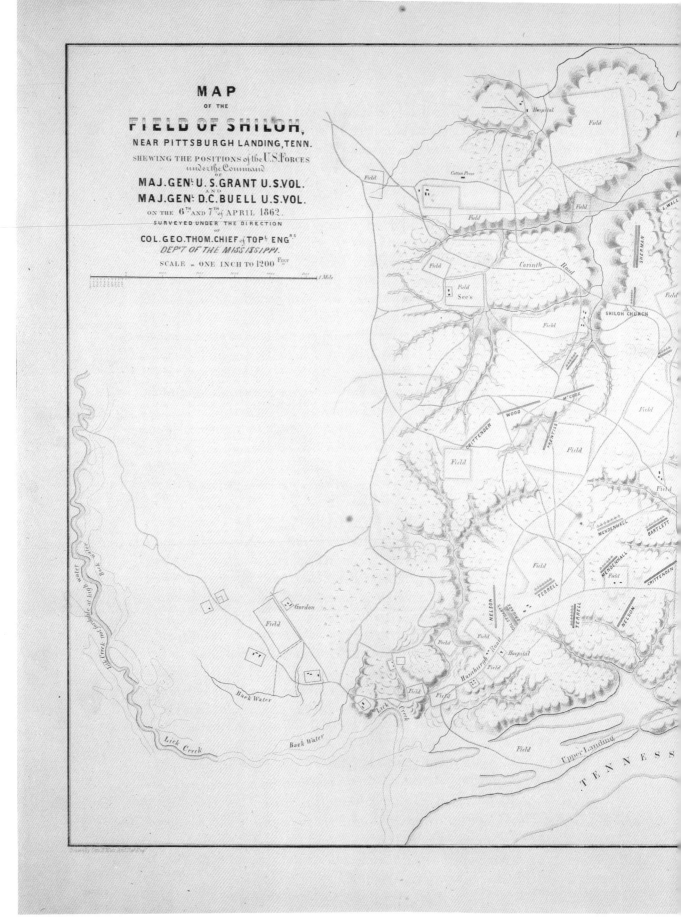

MAP
OF THE
FIELD OF SHILOH,
NEAR PITTSBURGH LANDING, TENN.
SHEWING THE POSITIONS of the U.S. FORCES
under the Command
OF
MAJ. GEN.ᴸ U. S. GRANT U.S.VOL.
AND
MAJ. GEN.ᴸ D.C. BUELL U.S.VOL.
ON THE 6ᵀᴴ AND 7ᵀᴴ of APRIL 1862.
SURVEYED UNDER THE DIRECTION
OF
COL. GEO. THOM. CHIEF of TOP.ᴸ ENG.ᴿˢ
DEP'T OF THE MISSISSIPPI.

SCALE = ONE INCH TO 1200 FEET

1 Mile

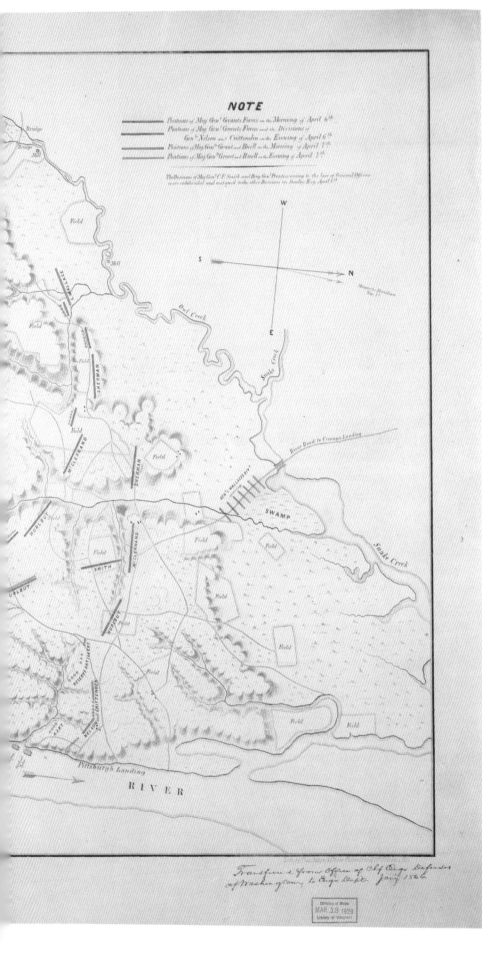

Assistant Topographical Engineer Otto H. Matz prepared this map of the battlefield at Shiloh for his superior officer, Colonel George Thom. Matz indicated the positions of Grant's and Buell's Union forces during the bloody two-day battle, but omitted their Confederate opponents.

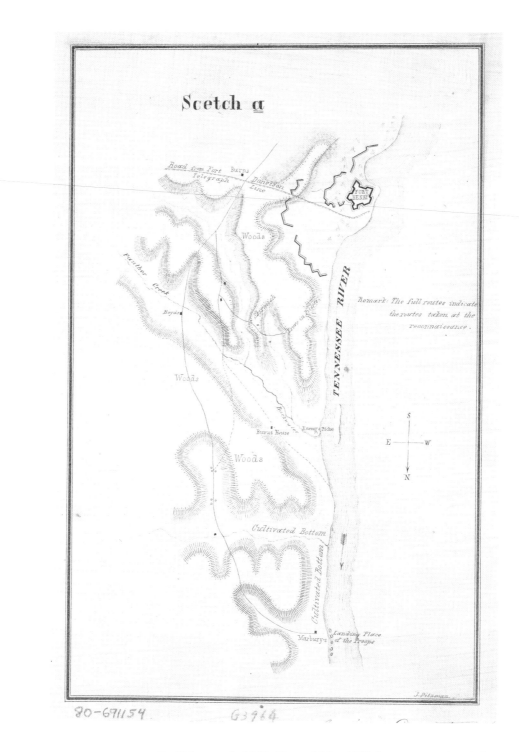

Scetch α

On February 6, 1862, General Lloyd Tilghman surrendered the
Tennessee River bastion of Fort Henry following a close-range
bombardment by Admiral Foote's Federal gunboats. Lieutenant Julius
Pitzman, a volunteer serving with the U.S. Topographical Engineers,
prepared this map of the fort's land approaches.

day," Sherman opened, to which Grant shot back, "Yes, lick 'em tomorrow though."

The following morning, April 7, it was the Confederates' turn to be surprised, as most of the army had gone to bed in the captured Union camps, and were eating for the first time in two days when Grant's counterattack slammed into them. The only Rebel not surprised was Colonel Nathan Bedford Forrest, who had accurately observed the arrival of Buell's advance elements, and predicted that if the Confederates didn't keep up the attack, they "would be whipped like hell by 10 o'clock tomorrow." Forrest was wrong by about five hours.

With Buell's reinforcements, Grant was able to throw 45,000 men against Beauregard's exhausted 20,000 and because the Confederates had expected a Union retreat, few units had bothered to refill their cartridge pouches. But in a reversal of the previous day's fight, the desperate Confederates repeatedly counter-charged the attacking Union masses. Despite no particularly sophisticated plans on Grant's part, his army soon was pressing back around Shiloh Church, reclaiming Sherman's old camps. At 3:30 that afternoon, Forrest's bitter prediction came true.

The Shiloh armies had been about twice the size of the forces at Bull Run, but they suffered more than five times the casualties. Precise numbers were never agreed upon, but each army had more than

"Furlough"
by Charles W. Reed.

Furlough

1,700 men killed and 8,000 wounded. The Federals listed 2,885 missing or captured, while the retreating Confederates claimed 959 missing. As in many Civil War battles, the victor failed to have a ready mobile reserve to follow up and consolidate his advantage with a vigorous pursuit and the loser escaped to fight again. The leadership on each side had been personally brave, but historians came to call Shiloh a "soldier's battle," reflecting the heroism of individual soldiers and regimental officers rather than any brilliance by the high command.

Because the South retreated, the North could and did claim victory. While Grant was the victor, his reputation suffered for the obvious surprise he and Sherman had allowed to happen. Rumors of drinking that followed Grant throughout the war were circulated, and led to one of the war's most enduring stories, when Lincoln supposedly responded to a request to sack him with "I can't spare this man, he fights." In fact, Halleck actually did push Grant aside. Only Sherman's personal plea kept Grant with the army, and only Halleck's subsequently bumbling, though successful, campaign against Corinth, Mississippi brought Grant back to field command.

With the capture of Corinth, Shiloh moved from a tactical to a strategic victory, as the campaign, which began at Forts Henry and Donelson, opened the road to eventual Union triumph in Kentucky and Tennessee, and paved the way for Grant's Vicksburg Campaign, which literally split the Confederacy and regained the Mississippi for the Union.

———— ✺ ————

After taking Forts Henry and Donelson, Grant moved his army down the Tennessee River to Pittsburg Landing. Grant believed that after their defeats at the upriver forts, the Confederates were demoralized and retreating, and so his main concern upon reaching the landing was finding adequate routes from the river to the Memphis and Charleston Railroad. These roads were not well marked on his map, so he organized reconnaissances to determine the best routes. His chief of staff, Colonel J.D. Webster, understood that the road from Eastport was a good one, but easy to ambush. On April 4th, in the same report in which Grant stated: "I have scarcely the faintest idea of an attack... being made upon us, but will be prepared should such a thing take place," he also reported his decision that he would use the road from Hamburg to Corinth (four miles up the Tennessee River) as his approach road to Corinth. Grant singled out his chief engineer, Lieutenant Colonel J.B. McPherson (later Major General and commander of this army during the Atlanta Campaign) for special praise because:

"All the grounds beyond our camps for miles have been reconnoitered by him and plats carefully prepared under his supervision give accurate information of the nature of approaches to our lines."

Grant's overconfidence was shattered by the Confederate attack, which pushed the Union troops in successive lines back towards the safety of their gunboats on the Tennessee. This can be seen on the Matz map (pp. 42-43) as the Union lines around Shiloh Church (solid blue lines) are pushed back to their afternoon positions towards the Tennessee River (white-blue-white bars).

There were two other instances in which maps were influential during the battle. First, General Don Carlos Buell reported when trying to reach Pittsburg Landing:

"My entire ignorance of the various roads and of the character of the country at the time rendered it impossible to anticipate the probable dispositions of the enemy."

The other mapping failure (or excuse) was with General Lew Wallace's "Lost Division." The general took nine hours (11:00 A.M. to 8:00 P.M.) to move his division from Crump's Landing to the right flank of the army, a distance of 5.5 miles, stating that his guides misled him. His division can also be seen on the Matz map as the column crossing Owl Creek on the right-hand edge (white-blue-white bars). Neither Grant nor his staff accepted that excuse, and Wallace was later brought before a Court of Inquiry for his conduct during the battle.

Chapter 3

Jackson In The Valley

Thomas Jonathan Jackson got his nickname at First Manassas, in northern Virginia, but he defined himself for history in the summer of 1862 in the Valley of Virginia, along the Shenandoah River and through the Blue Ridge Mountains.

The strategic goal of Jackson's Valley Campaign, as it came to be known, was to keep the massive Federal armies of the East from combining to crush Richmond. The capital of the Confederacy was in great peril that spring and summer as George McClellan was preparing to launch nearly 100,000 well-trained and properly equipped Federals against less than half that number of Confederate defenders, under Joseph E. Johnston.

But Jackson knew the Valley well by then, and he had trained his men to march and fight beyond what they thought were their capacities. So when Robert E. Lee, then serving as Jefferson Davis's military advisor, suggested that it would be critical for Jackson to somehow divert the Federals' attention, perhaps even to prevent the dispatch of more troops to McClellan's already huge army, Jackson was ready.

The degree to which Stonewall Jackson's character shaped the results of the Valley Campaign cannot be exaggerated. His troops came to admire him, and to expect miracles of him, and he of them. But he also came to terrify them, as well as the Federals and their commanders. His persistent ability to confuse and surprise occupied and diverted Lincoln and Secretary of War Edwin Stanton precisely when they should have kept their attention on the main chance to achieve victory: McClellan and his campaign.

Jackson was born in what was to become West Virginia, and graduated from West Point more by sheer determination than academic brilliance. He served in Mexico with distinction as a junior officer, then resigned from the army to become a professor of mathematics at the Virginia Military Institute.

There Jackson developed a well-deserved reputation as an eccentric man, and as a dry, rigid, humorless pedagogue. Jackson was deeply religious, even for the age. Of average height, he wore a size 14 shoe. In uniform, he sometimes resembled a large pair of boots in a coat, although no one who saw into his cold, light blue eyes felt like laughing. Even so, the daring and imagination he brought to his Civil War career astonished those who had known him at VMI.

After instant fame at First Manassas, Jackson's career through the winter of 1861-62 was undistinguished. Given command of the Shenandoah, he nearly destroyed his small army with forced marches through severe winter storms, only to fail against Federal detachments at Bath and Romney.

He lost the tactical fight at Kernstown, and blamed defeat on a subordinate, setting a pattern of high expectations and a lack of forgiveness to those whom he felt didn't measure up. While the odds said he would have lost in any event, Jackson wasted many lives by rushing in without proper scouting or support. But strategically, his 3,000-man attack against 9,000 Federals had enormous consequences: it set the precedent for Lincoln's attempts to micro-manage his Valley military, and prevented the first of many attempts to transfer Federal forces to McClellan.

Unfortunately the Union, Lincoln's Valley Army commander, Major General Nathaniel Banks, was a politician with no military experience, who at that time prided himself on neither consulting maps nor carefully scouting in advance. Banks did, of course, appreciate the military significance of Winchester, the largest town and transportation junction in the region. Banks had been Speaker of the U.S. House of Representatives and Governor of Massachusetts. He was a genuine patriot, and Lincoln was stuck with him, particularly at this point, when it looked like he was pursuing a defeated Stonewall Jackson.

Another effect of Jackson's initiative at Kernstown was that it prompted Lincoln to order General John C. Frémont, the western explorer and Republican presidential candidate in 1856, to come from western Virginia to cooperate with Banks in the Valley, rather than carrying out a personal scheme to liberate eastern Tennessee. And from the east, Lincoln ordered Irvin McDowell's Corps at Fredericksburg to move into the Valley to cut off Jackson from that direction, instead of moving south to join McClellan.

But if Jackson felt pressed from three sides, he didn't show it. Rather, he called in a 34-year-old schoolteacher from New York,

Jedediah Hotchkiss, Stonewall Jackson's brilliant topographer, mapped one of Jackson's rare military failures: the March 23, 1862 battle of Kernstown. Jackson placed blame for the Confederate defeat on General Richard B. Garnett, who withdrew the Stonewall Brigade at a critical moment in the fighting.

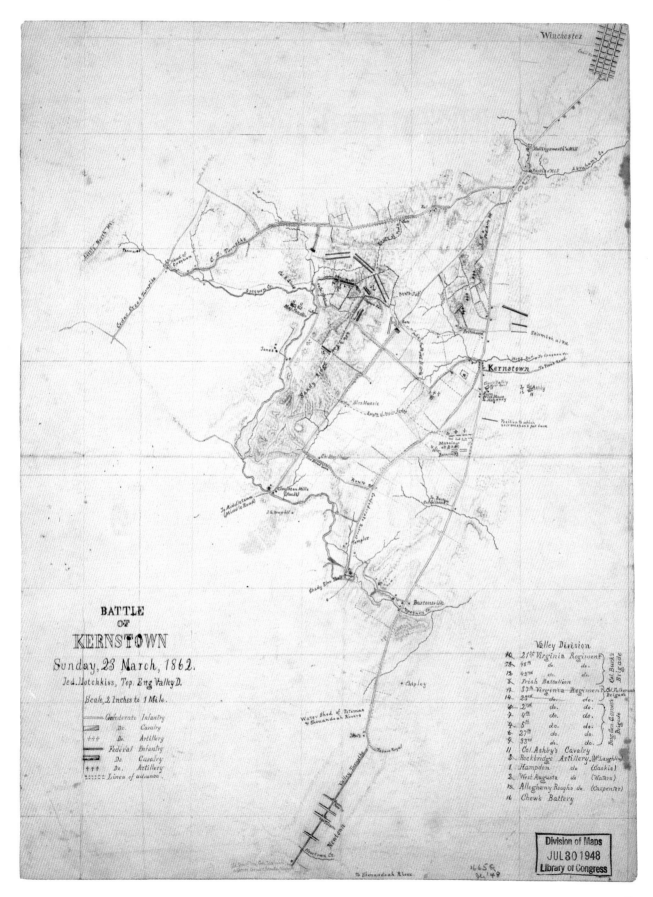

BATTLE
OF
KERNSTOWN

Sunday, 23 March, 1862.

Jed. Hotchkiss, Top. Eng. Valley D.

Scale, 2 Inches to 1 Mile.

———— Confederate Infantry
———— Do.   Cavalry
+++   Do.   Artillery
▬▬▬▬ Federal Infantry
▬▬▬▬ Do.   Cavalry
+++   Do.   Artillery
······· Lines of advance.

Valley Division

10.	21st Virginia Regiment		Col. Burks's Brigade
13.	48th do. do.		
12.	42nd do. do.		
8.	Irish Battalion		
17.	37th Virginia Regiment		Col. Fulkerson's Brigade
14.	23rd do. do.		
3.	2nd do. do.		Brig. Gen. Garnett's Brigade
7.	4th do. do.		
4.	5th do. do.		
6.	27th do. do.		
9.	33rd do. do.		
11.	Col. Ashby's Cavalry		
5.	Rockbridge Artillery (McLaughlin)		
1.	Hampden do. (Caskie)		
2.	West Augusta do. (Waters)		
15.	Alleghany Roughs do. (Carpenter)		
16.	Chew's Battery		

Sketch by Charles W. Reed.

Jedediah Hotchkiss, who had perfected his prewar avocation, making maps. Hotchkiss had long lived in the Shenandoah Valley, and considered it his homeland. Jackson gave him the following orders: "I want you to make me a map of the Valley, showing all the points of offense and defense. Mr. Pendleton will give you orders for whatever outfit you want. Good morning, Sir." And with that, Jackson took the one single step that enabled him to conceptualize and carry out what became known as his Valley Campaign.

Throughout the spring and early summer, Hotchkiss mapped almost the entire Valley, and was constantly at Jackson's side with local intelligence the Federal commanders lacked. Critical factors in the campaign's early stages were the inexperience of the Federal cavalry, and the superb guerilla war capabilities of Jackson's troopers, under General Turner Ashby. Unfortunately for Jackson, Ashby and his men rejected military discipline and frequently failed to rise above raiding, rather than helping to consolidate Jackson's victories.

Jackson's great campaign began with him in apparent flight from three converging Union armies. In reality, Jackson was in a race to defeat each army separately, "in detail," as the military called it, and his first target was the erratic Frémont. The "Pathfinder" of the early West was moving toward Jackson as slowly as he could without being removed from command by an increasingly furious Lincoln. The result was that Jackson sped down the macadamized Valley Turnpike, avoiding a planned ambush by all Federal forces.

Banks had been equally deliberate in his pursuit, and on April 22 actually telegraphed Washington that Jackson had "abandoned the Valley of Virginia permanently." Jackson's plan to mystify the enemy was working beyond expectation, and he moved to compound the confusion. Jackson marched his army down the Valley and apparently away from Staunton, Frémont's target, then doubled back using the railroad to surprise and defeat a smaller detachment of Frémont's army under General Robert Milroy, at McDowell, on May 8.

General Lee, still advising from Richmond, saw the possibilities presented by Jackson's initiative. Lee suggested that Jackson cooperate with General Richard Ewell's 8,500-man army, waiting at Stanardsville, north of Charlottesville, in case they were needed at

Richmond. Ewell and Jackson eagerly agreed, as this gave them a combined force of 17,000, enough to take on Banks. Ewell had to wait an agonizing three weeks at Swift Run Gap before Jackson's victory at McDowell freed the infantry, now known as "Jackson's Foot Cavalry," for their dash toward Winchester, and Banks.

Banks waited at Strasburg, convinced that Front Royal was a diversion, and that he was blocking Jackson's advance. Finally, the able Colonel George Gordon convinced Banks that despite his fears of the political costs (to him) of a retreat, if he didn't hurry back to Winchester he would be cut off entirely. Jackson spent the night by General Richard Taylor's campfire, contemplating which of several options Banks might choose. Ruling out an attempt by Banks to join forces with Frémont, Jackson decided to strike the Union army at Middletown, on the Valley Pike, to prevent Banks from reaching Winchester and its road network.

The plan worked perfectly, as Jackson's artillery blew apart men, wagons, and horses, while Wheat's Tigers charged in to help finish the job. But here the New Orleans roustabouts' lack of discipline

Stonewall Jackson's opponents in the Shenandoah Valley included the division commanded by Brigadier General Louis Blenker (left of center, gloved hand on belt). Blenker had emigrated to the United States from Germany after the failed revolution of 1848, and most of his troops were likewise foreign-born.
LC USZ62-92594

stalled Jackson's advance; the men fell to looting the wagons, and Banks gained enough time to reach defensive positions on the outskirts of Winchester.

The next day, May 25, Jackson planned to send his old Stonewall Brigade to lead the army against Banks's right flank. Ewell, on his own initiative, staged a simultaneous flank attack from the left. It was a complete success, as the Federal lines bent, then broke. An uncharacteristically ecstatic Jackson, shouting "The battle's won, now let's hollar," waved his cap and charged into Winchester with his men.

Banks and his army started running, and in fourteen hours from the start of Jackson's attack traveled thirty-five miles to the Potomac, and safety. Banks's army might have been captured, but Ashby's cavalry, ignoring orders and discipline as usual, were off raiding in the countryside and missed their opportunity. As it was, Banks lost more than one-third of his force; some 3,500 men were killed, wounded or captured.

Winchester was a victory of strategic importance, as it deepened the panic in Washington, and caused Lincoln to cancel transfer of McDowell's 40,000 men to McClellan, a move "Little Mac" came to blame for the defeat of his whole campaign. But Jackson wasn't done yet, as Frémont had

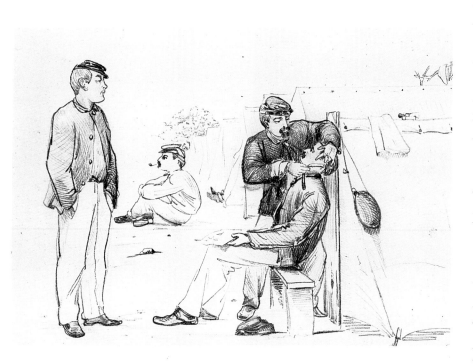

Charles Reed's depiction of a leisurely shaving break.

finally bestirred himself, and was moving into the southern end of the Valley in hopes of cutting Jackson off from Richmond. Remaining in the field were General James Shields and his men, not recalled to McDowell's army and still tasked with bringing Jackson to bay.

Lincoln became convinced that Jackson's victory at Winchester was the portent of an attack on Washington itself, and that he had to devise a trap for Jackson, because his generals seemed incapable of it. While Lincoln's plans were basically sound, they depended on separate and uncoordinated commanders for execution. Frémont was to chase Jackson via the north fork of the Shenandoah; Shields would follow the south fork, in hopes of cutting Jackson off.

McDowell was to bring up the rear.

While Shields had already proven himself capable at Kernstown, Frémont continually failed to move in time, and in the end, Lincoln's trap turned into a two-pronged pursuit. Jackson had no intention of allowing his enemies to unite against him, and moved as rapidly along the Valley Pike as the "Foot Cavalry" could go.

Jackson was still in danger of being cut off by Frémont and Shields if they united, something Jackson forestalled by burning all the bridges save one at Port Republic, which he might need for his own retreat. Jackson had barely reached the town on June 7 when he was nearly captured by cavalry from Shields's division. Shields's men also failed to burn the bridge, which Jackson promptly secured. Now that the pursuing Federals were divided by the river, Jackson calculated that his best chance was to block the hapless Frémont the next day, at Cross Keys, before turning on Shields.

Ewell's division of 6,500 thus faced Frémont's 15,000, but Frémont used only five of the twenty-four regiments in his army against the Confederates. Even more inexcusably, Frémont managed only a single serious push against Ewell's lines. The Yankees involved fought hard but were thrown back. Given the great disparity of forces, Jackson and Ewell didn't dare move from the defensive until they had driven off Shields. But it is indicative of the character of the Confederates that they were angry and frustrated by Frémont's failure to make a serious attempt against them. Tactically, it was a critical victory for Jackson, as Ewell could now leave a small blocking force to face Frémont, while the two of them turned on Shields the next day, June 9.

But at this point, Jackson almost repeated his failure against Shields at Kernstown back in March. In his eagerness to get on with a renewed attack on Frémont, Jackson sent the Stonewall Brigade against Shields's lines without properly scouting the position, and without bringing up adequate support.

The Confederates ran headlong into a nasty surprise of well-placed infantry and artillery firing down on them from a spur of the mountain used for making coal, guarded by an apparently impenetrable woods. The Stonewall Brigade was close to being trapped at "The Coaling" when it was rescued by one of Richard Taylor's Louisiana regiments. The Federals counterattacked, and it seemed certain that Taylor and the Stonewall Brigade would be captured when forces led by Richard Ewell himself came crashing out of the woods to take the position, and the guns, for the South.

Shields's main force stayed down on the plain by the river. When more Confederate reinforcements arrived, the Federals concluded

Brigadier General Richard Taylor, the son of Mexican War hero and U.S. President Zachary Taylor, commanded a brigade of hard-fighting Louisianans that helped win the day for Stonewall Jackson's army at the battle of Port Republic. LC B8172-2113

Battle of Winchester at the stone wall

Deployed in an elbow-to-elbow line of battle typical of Civil War tactics, soldiers of the 84th Pennsylvania charge a stone wall defended by Jackson's Confederates at the battle of Kernstown. The engagement was a Northern victory, but cost the Pennsylvania unit 71 wounded and 21 killed; among the latter was their commanding officer, Colonel William G. Murray.
LC USZ62-7003

A sketch by Charles Reed of camp life.

they had done enough, and retreated. But it had been a near run thing, and for Jackson, a poorly managed fight which could have gone to the Union. When it was over, Jackson turned to Ewell and said "He who does not see the hand of God in this is blind, sir, blind."

John C. Frémont watched Shields retire from bluffs across the river, fired some parting artillery shells and retreated to Harrisonburg, then on to Mt. Jackson. Shields pulled his men all the way back to Luray. Jackson waited in the Valley for a few days, and when the Federals showed no further inclination for trouble, the campaign, Jackson's Valley Campaign, ended.

From the first fight at Kernstown in March, Jackson had marched up and down the Valley for six battles, winning four tactically, and losing none strategically. He had demoralized three Federal armies, admittedly poorly led, not to mention Lincoln and Stanton, and caused them to withhold some 60,000 Union soldiers who might otherwise have been brought to bear on Richmond.

On June 23, Jackson made a secret visit to Richmond, and rashly promised he would have his entire army in place against McClellan within twenty-four hours. By then, Robert E. Lee had assumed command of what became known as the Army of Northern Virginia, and he and Jackson would fight together for a year. Jackson never returned to the Valley.

⟨〰〰〰⟩

Jackson is rightly recognized as one of the best map consumers of the Civil War. Not only did he recognize their importance, but he understood the commander's role in directing what should be mapped as Richard Stephenson has discussed on page ten. Frequently, Civil War commanders gave their topographers little guidance about what to map (McClellan is a good example). Although Jackson was often a secretive commander, he gave

Hotchkiss definite instructions for mapping, which Hotchkiss carried out with talent and vigor.

Jackson was also very much at home in the Shenandoah Valley so Hotchkiss's efforts were complemented by Jackson's personal knowledge. Stonewall began his campaign with an attack against superior forces at Kernstown on March 23, 1862. The crucial geographic feature of the valley was the Valley Pike, the macadamized road seen on the right side of the Hotchkiss map (p.49). This battle actually took place off to the left center, on the hills which commanded the area. It was here, at the base of the hills, where the 84th Pennsylvania charged Jackson's troops (pp. 54-55), an attack which forced Confederate General Richard Garnett to order the retreat of Stonewall's brigade. Jackson blamed Garnett for the defeat and had him removed.

Jackson's first important advantage accruing from maps occurred in early May when he marched his division through Brown's Gap, away from the valley, as if he were going to reinforce Richmond. Ten miles short of Charlottesville, his troops boarded cars on the Virginia Central Railroad and headed back into the valley. They marched through Staunton and joined Edward Johnson for the successful attack against Brigadier General Milroy at McDowell.

The second, and more important, Confederate map advantage was the crucial New Market Gap over the Massanutton Mountain. After beating Milroy at McDowell, Jackson marched down the macadamized Valley Pike, then at New Market he cut across the mountain into the Luray Valley. When he fell upon Union General Banks's flank guard at Front Royal, he had achieved complete surprise.

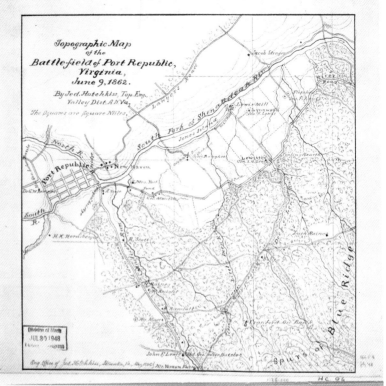

Jedediah Hotchkiss's manuscript map of the battle of Port Republic.

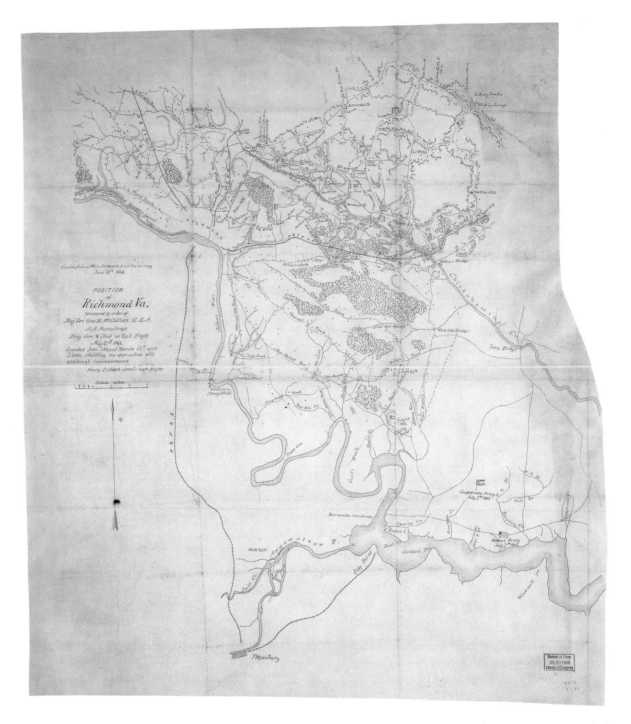

West Point educated Lieutenant Henry Lorcom Abbott prepared a detailed survey of the Richmond vicinity for the Army of the Potomac's Chief Topographical Engineer, General Andrew A. Humphreys. Small Union and Confederate flags mark where battles occurred during McClellan's "change of base" from the York to the James River.

Chapter 4

On the Peninsula

*T*he role of the Civil War in America's national mythology has tended to pasteurize the dishonesties and political failures that produced it. So it is hard today to recapture the depth of passion and fear that motivated the people of the North and South, and their politicians, newspaper editors, and soldiers.

Such postwar myths as "The Lost Cause" and the patriotic unity of North and South, respectively, have much truth at their roots, of course, but they obscure the fact that the Civil War was produced and characterized by irrational extremes of misguided patriotism, hatred, and mistrust.

A civil war by definition is a time of divided loyalties, fear and paranoia; it is fought against the enemy without, and the enemy within. The American Civil War was created, and then prolonged far beyond what basic military realities could have predicted, by the politics of emotion and, particularly in the North, an irrational search for treason. Never was this more obvious, nor more debilitating to the war effort, than in events leading up to the Union's grand assault against Richmond in the summer of 1862.

In fact, many of the failures of Major General George B. McClellan that summer can be traced to a small unit action on the shores of the Potomac River, near Leesburg, Virginia, in October of 1861. Ball's Bluff was a small battle with huge consequences, as its political resonance often had a near-paralyzing effect on Union commanders well through the Battle of Gettysburg.

What happened at Ball's Bluff, a costly and dramatic Federal defeat, isn't as important as what the radical faction of the Republican Party in Congress thought happened. The fact that a popular former senator, Colonel Edward D. Baker, a close friend of Lincoln's, was killed added spice to the zeal for scapegoats and conspiracies which spurred the Committee on the Conduct of the War from Ball's Bluff until the final surrender in 1865.

The congressmen became convinced there was a conspiracy of some kind in the cadre of West Point graduates attempting to lead the Union Army against Confederates led by former classmates, and in many cases close friends. The fact that most professional Union generals were Democrats also created problems, as the Democrats were seen as less aggressive and more accommodating toward the South than Republicans. The fact that Lincoln's personal views and goals at this point mirrored those of the Democrats' caused the Committee members to feel all the more their burden for ensuring the triumph of liberty.

After hearings on Ball's Bluff, which resembled those of the French Revolution, a Union general was jailed without trial or formal charges, and was disgraced in the press. The loyalty and competence of the professional officer corps was repeatedly questioned by the committee and its partisan press allies. McClellan and other Union generals were inadvertently taught the object lesson that success didn't count so much as avoiding failure. Failure might mean not simply a great loss of life by troops, but even a loss of personal freedom and reputation by the leader.

It is impossible to judge the behavior of McClellan and the Union generals until the advent of Grant without considering the cancerous effect of Congress second-guessing their command decisions. In Jackson's Valley Campaign, the fetid political atmosphere caused Lincoln and his new Secretary of War, Edwin Stanton, to micro-manage the Union's response to Jackson's diversionary efforts.

Mistrust of McClellan grew during his months of delay through 1861 in order to properly train and equip the post-Bull Run army. McClellan became increasingly arrogant, and never grasped the politics inherent in the war. Lincoln's frustrations rose to the point where he and his cabinet tried to direct the army's campaign against the Confederates, still dug-in by the Manassas battlefield and commanded by Joseph Johnston.

It was during this period that McClellan, for all of his flaws, performed his lasting contribution to the Union's final victory: he created almost out of his own will the Army of the Potomac; he taught its officers how to organize and lead; he taught the men how to believe in themselves and in the army. None of McClellan's failures in the field shook this basic faith, which enabled the men to endure and then win the war in the East.

In early 1862 McClellan realized he had to get going or lose his command, and his plan was excellent: outflank Johnston by water to Urbana, on the Rappahannock River, via the Chesapeake Bay, and drive on to Richmond. It might have worked had not Johnston retreated, as he would in every campaign he fought through the war. Lincoln and Stanton also behaved characteristically, demanding that McClellan detail large numbers of troops to guard Washington, despite the impossibility of a serious Confederate assault while simultaneously defending Richmond against McClellan. Lincoln's concerns predated Jackson's activities and continued well into 1864 under Grant.

Lincoln's fears must be placed in the context of the military intelligence failures that so paralyzed McClellan in all of his campaigns: wanting to believe, perhaps, he readily accepted reports that Johnston's army at Manassas had 100,000 to 200,000 men. Though embarrassed by Johnston's retreat, McClellan revised his plan to what is now called the

Peninsula Campaign, moving the entire army 200 miles by boat to land at Fortress Monroe, where the Chesapeake Bay meets the James River. This attack again outflanked Johnston, who had only fallen back to Fredericksburg.

The whole scheme was almost stopped in early March by the scare of the CSS Virginia, the world's first successful ironclad naval vessel. But in the March 9 *Monitor-Merrimac* battle, which introduced a new class of warships to the world, McClellan's water-borne supply lines were secured.

On April 4, McClellan started his push up the peninsula created by the James and York rivers. On his maps, it seemed a relatively easy route, because they utterly failed to show the many small streams and swamps that made the peninsula, in fact, a very difficult route indeed. He was also misinformed about the consistency of the roads, which weren't the sandy, firm paths predicted, but virtually bottomless red mud following the spring rains. And the roads rarely ran where shown, nor were all shown on the maps. Lastly, McClellan ran into an excellent Confederate defensive line thrown up by

At 35, Major General George B.McClellan (fourth from right) found himself entrusted with command of the largest army ever assembled on the American continent. His unsurpassed managerial skills and personal rapport with the men in the ranks forged an efficient fighting force, but McClellan's campaign on the Virginia Peninsula was characterized by overcaution and lost opportunities. LC B8184-10111

General John Magruder. It ran along the Warwick River, guarding Yorktown, site of the British surrender to George Washington, ending what the South called the First American Revolution.

In less than a month, McClellan carried out the transfer of 120,000 soldiers, 15,000 horses and mules, 1,100 wagons, 74 ambulances, and everything needed to sustain this vast army aimed at the heart of the Confederacy. Even with the natural obstacles, the campaign should have succeeded. The entire Rebel army in Virginia totaled just over half of McClellan's force, now 70 miles from Richmond.

McClellan's plan was to push rapidly up the York River to West Point, a natural base for the final drive on Richmond. Facing him along the Yorktown line were Magruder's 17,000 with orders to hold on long enough to allow Johnston's 60,000 to race down from Fredericksburg.

But Stonewall Jackson supplied a nasty surprise when McClellan was told upon landing that a key part of his strategy, 40,000 Federals of Irvin McDowell's army, would be held back to defend Washington. McDowell was his strategic reserve, to be thrown into battle at the critical point. Lincoln and Stanton promised that as soon as possible, some or all would be released, and McClellan went on. But the McDowell promise came to dictate McClellan's conduct of the campaign, and provided the key to Confederate victory.

Magruder, known as "Prince John" to friends, loved amateur theatrics. At Yorktown, he employed the classic ruse of marching bodies of troops in large circles through clearings in the woods. McClellan and his scouts, believing themselves perhaps already outnumbered, didn't attack.

The delay gave the South time to move down Johnston's men; when McClellan finally pounced on Yorktown, the Confederates were headed for their main defensive lines at Williamsburg. By then, a frustrated and worried Lincoln had bombarded McClellan with preemptory orders to attack, further alienating the general from his political base. Williamsburg, the first serious fight of the campaign, was won when General Winfield Scott Hancock, disobeying orders to withdraw, launched a flank attack which routed Confederates under General Jubal Early. "Hancock was superb," McClellan reported. A junior officer who gained notice for capturing a battle flag was staff Captain George Armstrong Custer. McClellan now had his first victory and was just fifty miles from Richmond. The Confederates thought McClellan would be among them shortly, and panic set in. Arrangements were made to burn the city and evacuate the country's gold reserves. Many of the leading citizens, including President Davis, sent their families away. But Davis's military advisor, General Robert E. Lee, put backbone into the cabinet discussions by declaring "Richmond must not be given up! It shall not be given up!"

Lee's determination stiffened further on May 15 when the Union Navy failed to overcome Confederate artillery on Drewry's Bluff, near the city. McClellan's army was just twenty-three miles away, but advancing with such deliberation that General Philip Kearney wrote home sarcastically calling his commander the "Virginia creeper."

At this critical juncture, Lincoln and Stanton changed McClellan's plan of attack by announcing that they would, finally, release the bulk of McDowell's army. Rather than coming by the Chesapeake, as McClellan hoped, the reinforcements were to march south to guard against any sudden attack on Washington from that direction.

The strategic significance of this was that McClellan split his army, placing a wing across the Chickahominy River in preparation for a linkup with McDowell. McClellan had just reorganized his force into five army corps in preparation for the final attack on Richmond, south of the Chickahominy. Now, he sent three corps north of the river, with Major General Fitz John Porter's Fifth Corps extending to the right, toward Mechanicsville, six miles northeast of Richmond.

By May 24, McClellan's left wing was in place at the Seven Pines crossroads, just six miles east of Richmond. Union soldiers on each flank could hear church bells ringing in the city. At this point, Lincoln wired that because of Stonewall Jackson's heroics against Frémont and Shields, he was delaying McDowell's march indefinitely, but not canceling it. McClellan was left with his right flank out in the open, hoping that at some point it would be reinforced by McDowell. His immediate concern was the river itself, which was swollen to a twenty-year high by daily rains that had encumbered the army's wagons and artillery and slowed his entire advance.

On May 27, McClellan ordered Porter to further extend his flanks by destroying railroad tracks out as far as Hanover Court House, and clearing a path for McDowell's men to use

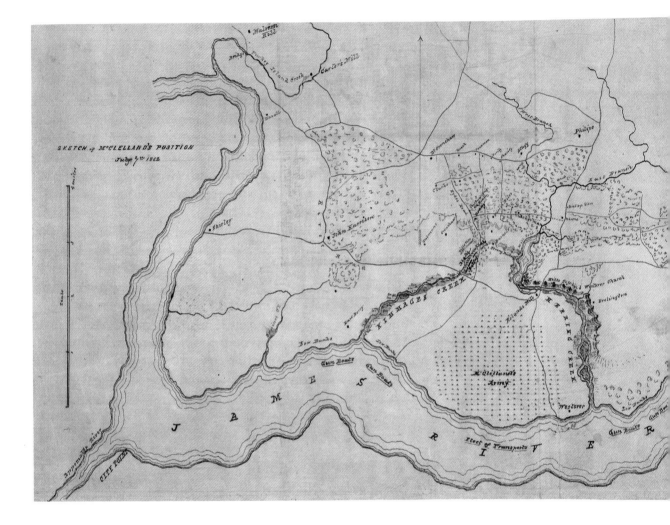

Though he misspelled the name of the Union commander, Confederate Captain William W. Blackford drew a generally accurate plan of McClellan's heavily defended position at Harrison's Landing. The James River plantation "Westover," visible at the lower right of the encampment, served as Federal headquarters.

whenever they arrived. A sharp fight produced a Union victory and caused Joe Johnston, ignorant of Lincoln's dilemma, to worry that McDowell's army might be coming close. Lincoln's anxiety and frustration were mirrored by those of Davis, Lee, and the people of Richmond, who couldn't understand Johnston's passivity in the face of McClellan's seemingly inexorable advance.

Johnston could see that he had run out of time, and planned to hit the Federal right wing at Mechanicsville on May 29, to forestall its junction with McDowell. But the night before the attack the Confederates learned that McDowell wasn't coming after all. Johnston then switched to a plan he had favored since McClellan split his army: attack the two exposed Union corps south of the Chickahominy near Seven Pines and defeat them before the Federals could be reunited across a few shaky bridges.

Johnston drew up an excellent plan, but everything went awry:

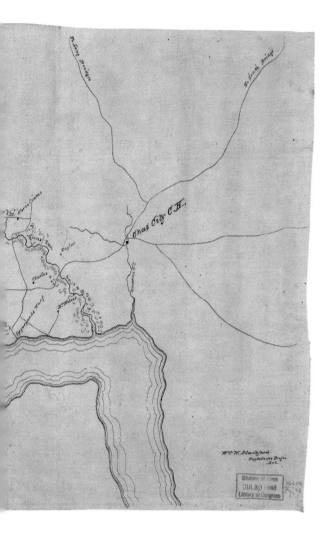

inexcusably, Johnston gave written orders to his lesser subordinates, but didn't tell them the overall plan. General James Longstreet, leading the main attack, got extensive oral orders, but nothing in writing. The attack was to have been launched on the morning of May 31 but the day began with Longstreet promptly taking the wrong road, and blocking the other units.

By 1 p.m. a frustrated General D.H. Hill attacked alone, and by 3 p.m. the desperate Federals were driven back to Seven Pines itself. As Philip Kearney came to a temporary rescue, Hill frantically asked Longstreet for reinforcements. Longstreet was still confused, and sent most to the wrong place. Finally, Confederates under General Micah Jenkins came crashing down Nine Mile Road and split the Federal forces between Seven Pines and Fair Oaks. Prompt action by Longstreet and Johnston could smash McClellan as planned.

Johnston, in the presence of Lee and Davis, who had come out to witness the fight, rode toward Seven Pines to do what Longstreet should have. But Johnston's luck was about to run out. In the evening, while scouting the front, he was struck by a musket ball in the shoulder and shrapnel in the chest, wounds which would debilitate him through the Vicksburg Campaign of 1863. Immediate command fell to General G.W. Smith, who, frozen by anxiety that McClellan was going to counterattack, let the opportunity slip.

The next morning, Longstreet quietly refused to follow Smith's flawed orders for renewed attack, and bitter but inconclusive fighting was finally called off by the new commander of the Confederate army, Robert E. Lee. The two- day battle at Seven Pines and Fair Oaks was the biggest in the East to that point: each side had roughly 41,000 men engaged, although the attacking Rebels lost a thousand more men than the Federals, with 6,134 killed, wounded, and missing.

McClellan had been ill prior to the battle, and in fact stayed in bed throughout it, not rousing himself until the Confederates were repulsed, when he rode out to accept the cheers of the men. But many officers, aware of how little McClellan had done to meet the emergency,

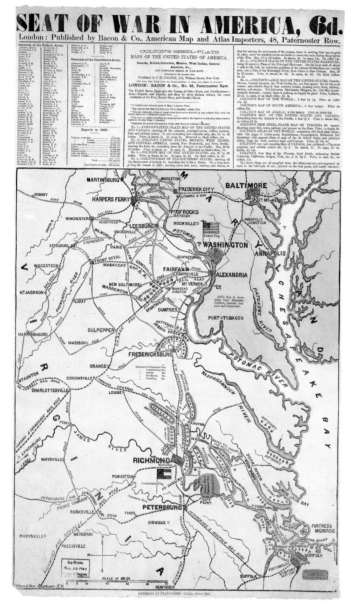

In July 1862 the London firm of Waters & Sons printed an overview of the "seat of war" in the eastern United States. Poised just southeast of Richmond, the position of George McClellan's Army of the Potomac is shaded red.

joined journalists in writing home and feeding the growing doubts about his abilities.

The battle left the two armies more or less in place, with the Federals pulled back slightly and dug in considerably. McClellan was still planning to attack, but wanted to bring up more supplies, more siege guns, and to wait for McDowell. He saw no need to rush. But Lee, until then a disappointment given his prewar record, took three weeks to reorganize and give a new name to the Army of Northern Virginia. Then he struck, and McClellan never again had the tactical initiative.

THE SEVEN DAYS

Great things had been expected of Robert E. Lee, ever since he declined Lincoln's offer to command Federal forces and went with his native Virginia. One of the Old Army's finest soldiers, Lee had graduated first in his class at West Point, been a dashing and distinguished staff officer in Mexico, and then a commandant at West Point, where he helped train many of the officers now opposing him.

Lee played something of a diplomat amongst the warring political factions and the fractious egos of his military colleagues. Unlike both Johnston and McClellan, Lee enjoyed the complete trust of his president. Like McClellan, Lee gained the trust and love of his army to a degree which, in fact, worked to the army's disadvantage later in the war.

But the main contrast between Lee and both Johnston and McClellan is that while the two always moved to conserve their men and their position, Lee always thought in terms of attack. Lee felt that given the Confederacy's limited resources, in the long run he could best conserve both men and position by denying the Federals the initiative.

In the present and most future contexts, this meant having his army on the move, either attacking or forcing an attack on favorable ground. While it staved off defeat, in the end Lee's strategy used up men who couldn't be replaced, and generals like U.S. Grant, who were just as audacious as he, beat him. But the summer of 1862 belonged to Robert E. Lee, and it began with his attack on McClellan on June 25, to start what became known as the Seven Days.

Lee made his move after sending Jeb Stuart's cavalry to see just how badly exposed McClellan's northern flanks were, as Porter's Fifth Corps awaited McDowell. In one of the war's great exploits Stuart humiliated McClellan by riding around his entire army and reentering Richmond from the south. In this triumph can be seen the seeds of Stuart's disaster in the Gettysburg Campaign. And while it gave Lee the intelligence he wanted, a more limited scout, as ordered, might not have so thoroughly alerted McClellan to the degree of his right flank's exposure.

At the time, Stuart gave the South a badly needed morale lift and by cutting McClellan's supply lines. As a result of this brash action McClellan's resolved to move his base and one more corps south of the Chickahominy. Lee decided to bring Stonewall Jackson from the Valley to attack Porter, while he and the main army swept along the north bank of the Chickahominy toward McClellan's main supply base at White House Landing.

McClellan also finally received some of McDowell's elusive army: 10,000 Pennsylvania Reserves under General George McCall, who arrived by boat. Reinforced, McClellan felt he could risk the offensive and planned a minor attack on June 26 to push his siege guns a mile closer to Richmond from the west. A small battle called Oak Grove thus began the Seven Days. It showed Lee what a risk he was taking, leaving General John Magruder with 25,000 men south of the Chickahominy to block McClellan's 60,000 man force while he concentrated on crushing Porter's 30,000 exposed Federals north of the river.

In that effort, Longstreet's 47,000 would be aided by what

British artist Frank Vizetelly sketched well-uniformed troopers of the 1st Virginia Cavalry, one of J.E.B. Stuart's hard-riding regiments. Stuart's daring ride around McClellan's army further intimidated the cautious Union commander, and helped set the stage for the Seven Days battles.
LC USZ62-157

Captain Horatio Gibson's battery of Union horse artillery assembles near the battlefield of Fair Oaks in June, 1862. Though the Federals suffered a strategic defeat in the Seven Days battles, their artillery proved more than a match for Robert E. Lee's gunners. Captain Gibson would be brevetted brigadier general for his wartime service.
LC B8171-431

Massive supplies of Federal ordnance, including stubby siege mortars and the larger Parrott guns, are stockpiled on the wharves at Yorktown, Virginia prior to the Army of the Potomac's advance against Richmond.
LC B8184-B82

Lee planned as a flank attack from the Shenandoah Valley by Stonewall Jackson's 18,500 "foot cavalry." Jackson had come down secretly to promise that his army would be in place for an attack on the morning of June 26.

But as the day wore on, an increasingly anxious Lee realized that even though McClellan was not attacking Magruder there was no sign of Longstreet's attack on Porter. A message from Jackson indicated a six hour delay, at least. At 3 p.m. General A.P. Hill, ordered to wait for Jackson's attack before launching his, assumed that Jackson must be approaching and pushed off without orders and without notifying Lee, who was only two miles away.

Hill crossed the Chickahominy and assaulted superior Union forces, well dug in at Mechanicsville, confident that the Federals would soon be taken in the flank by Jackson. At 5 p.m. Jackson came within two miles of Hill, and the musket fire of his fight could clearly be heard. Lee's plan was about to work. But then something quite extraordinary occurred: Stonewall Jackson, in sound of the guns, halted his army, pitched his tent, and went to sleep for the night.

Historians have professed to be mystified by Jackson's behavior then and throughout the Seven Days. At every opportunity Jackson failed, often appearing devoid of initiative or insensitive to the opportunities before him. In retrospect, there is little mystery. Jackson had exerted a superhuman effort of physical and mental activity since December of 1861; he had successfully waged the Valley Campaign; and then with ten hours of sleep in four days, rushed to the relief of Richmond. The mystery is not why he failed to perform, but why he did not collapse entirely.

Jackson's failure at Mechanicsville ended Lee's first battle of the Seven Days and cost the Confederates 1,500 in killed, wounded, and missing. But as McClellan was to discover, Lee was just starting to see what his men could do. The next day, the two armies collided again, at Gaines's Mill.

McClellan, still fearing he was outnumbered, planned to move his base to Harrison's Landing on the James. Seeing the Union pullback, Lee sent four columns after them. The Federals spent the day entrenched at Gaines's Mill, along Boatswain's Creek, where A.P. Hill's men ran into them. With Lee watching, Hill sent in his division at 2:30 p.m., both men confident that Longstreet would come up soon on the right, and that Jackson and D.H. Hill would appear on the left at any moment.

A.P. Hill's force took terrible casualties for nearly two hours before Lee pulled it back, as Longstreet had just arrived and there was no sign of Jackson. Finally, some of Richard Ewell's portion of the Valley Army reached the field and gained a foothold. At this point, Lee had 50,000 men against 30,000 and if the attack was pressed, the Union forces would collapse. Jackson finally ambled up, and Lee readied his combined armies for a grand assault at 7 p.m. By then Fitz John Porter had committed all his reserves and despite urgent pleas to McClellan, back in camp as usual, only two brigades were sent.

John Bell Hood's Texas Brigade led the Confederate breakthrough and Porter's line finally broke and ran. Porter had done a masterful job all day, but the numbers were against him, and Robert E. Lee had his first victory at the head of the Army of Northern Virginia. The cost to the South was terrible: 8,751 of the attacking 50,000 were killed or wounded, including large numbers of brigade and regimental commanders. The Confederates halted at dusk and the defeated Army of the Potomac successfully escaped across the Chickahominy.

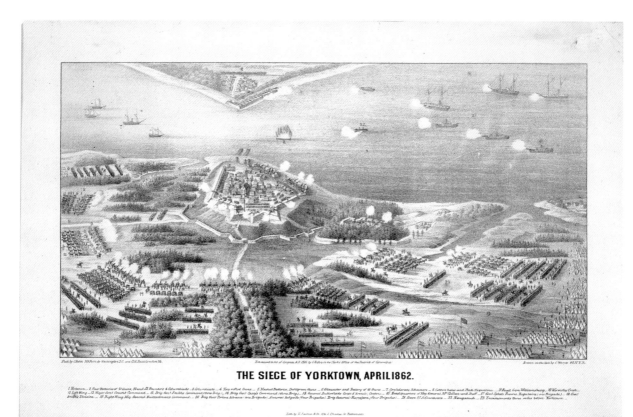

THE SIEGE OF YORKTOWN, APRIL 1862.

Arrayed with the rigid precision of toy soldiers, McClellan's Union forces surround the Confederate stronghold at Yorktown in this birds-eye view of the April, 1862 siege. Having successfully delayed the Federal advance up the Peninsula, General Magruder's Southern garrison evacuated Yorktown before "Little Mac" could launch an assault.

At this point, McClellan sent the following telegram to Secretary of War Stanton: "The Government has not sustained this army. If you do not do so now the game is lost. If I save this army now, I tell you plainly that I owe no thanks to you or to any other person in Washington. You have done your best to sacrifice this army." The Federal military censor couldn't believe what he was reading and actually softened McClellan's words before delivering the telegram. But Stanton and Lincoln soon learned of the original content, and their confidence in McClellan was further shaken.

After firing off his telegram McClellan called a late night meeting to discuss his other enemy, the Confederates. With Union pickets only four miles from Richmond, subordinates like Kearney argued for a renewed attack by a unified army. But McClellan, still convinced he faced 200,000 Rebels, stunned his commanders by announcing a retreat, which he called a "change of base," south to a new position on the James River. McClellan though t he was in a race to save his army. To do so would require a fight-inretreat back down the Peninsula with Lee at his heels. If McClellan won he would have a secure base to launch a renewed campaign against Richmond, and indeed that was his plan.

On June 29 a stiff rearguard action at Savage's Station easily drove off Magruder's troops, coming down the Williamsburg Road. The plan called for Jackson to join Magruder, but as throughout this campaign, the still-exhausted Jackson failed. This gave McClellan time to get across White Oak Swamp and head for the James and its Union gunboats ten miles away.

On June 30, Jackson again did not bring his troops into action as ordered, leaving Longstreet and A.P. Hill to waste two divisions in a bloody fight at Frayser's Farm. Confederate losses were 3,300 killed, wounded, or missing to the Federal's 2,800, mostly captured. The two lost opportunities by Lee gave McClellan time to dig into very strong positions on top of Malvern Hill, held by Porter's Fifth Corps.

July l saw Jackson come up with Lee for a commanders' conference at Glendale. Holding his temper in public, Lee responded to a remark that McClellan might yet escape, "Yes, he will get away because I cannot get my orders carried out!" In fact, Lee correctly guessed McClellan would make one last stand on Malvern Hill.

Previous battles had been lost by poor staff work and failures by subordinates, but the challenge facing Lee at Malvern Hill was straightforward: the Army of Northern Virginia was all in place.

Sketch by Charles W. Reed.

Bivouac at Gainsville
Oct 20 /68

It faced an insurmountable obstacle, however. Staring down at them were 250 Federal artillery pieces brought up by Colonel Henry Hunt.

Longstreet thought the Federal guns could be flanked by massed Confederate artillery firing from east and west, allowing an infantry assault up the middle. Lee agreed. By midafternoon, Lee realized a frontal assault couldn't work and began looking for a way to hit the flanks. But when some Federal troop redeployments were misinterpreted by watching Confederates, Lee ordered Magruder's 15,000 men to make their previously intended grand assault. Once again staff work failed and confusion resulted in only 5,000 rushing into the massed Federal artillery, unsupported by Confederate counterfire.

D.H. Hill heard the musketry of Magruder's men, assumed that the grand assault was working, and led what turned into a suicidal charge around 7 p.m. up the Willis Church Road, on the Union right. A single Union battery fired 1,392 rounds and then chopped up its guncarriage chains to rip into the Confederates. Darkness halted the fight. Lee had lost 5,255 killed and wounded to the Federals' less than 3,000.

Lee saved Richmond in the Seven Days, but McClellan reached his new base at Harrison's Landing, on the James, saving the Army of the Potomac for other days. The cost to the Confederates was one out of every four men in Lee's army, some 20,000 killed, wounded, or missing, including ten brigade and sixty-six regimental commanders.

Lee pulled back to Richmond to rest, refit, and plan his invasion of Maryland and Pennsylvania. McClellan sulked at Harrison's Landing for a month, pleading for reinforcements. But Lincoln had had enough: McClellan and his army were brought home August 3. Lee and Lincoln focused on a new Federal Army, led by General John Pope, which was moving rapidly into northern Virginia from Washington. The South could barely replace Lee's losses. Lincoln called for 300,000 new volunteers, and they came.

—⊂∰⊃—

The Peninsula between the York and James Rivers had not been well mapped before the War. After McClellan's original plan to land at Urbana was discarded, he was forced to turn to the alternate route from Fortress Monroe (see picture in Chapter 1) and up the Peninsula.

The map he used for the early campaign was a bad one compiled by Colonel Thomas Jefferson Cram in late 1861. On this map, an entire river was plotted incorrectly (see page 61), which led McClellan to later declare:

"In the commencement of the movement from Fort Monroe serious difficulties were encountered from the want of precise topographical information as to the country, in advance. Correct local maps were not to be found, and the country, though known in its general features, we found to be inaccurately described in essential particulars in the only maps and geographical memoirs or papers to which access could be had. Erroneous courses to streams and roads were frequently given, and no dependence could be placed on the information thus derived. This difficultly has been found to exist with respect to most portions of the State of Virginia through which my military operations have extended."

Ironically, the North did have a good map of Henrico County (Richmond), so the closer the Union Army got to Richmond, the better their maps became! In addition, the Union army had a large topographic staff, under Captain (later Major General) Andrew A. Humphreys who supplemented this information with some excellent surveying work behind the lines. This work greatly aided McClellan's change of base from the York to the James River (p. 58).

The Confederate map situation was just as bad as the Union's had been in the early campaign. Although General Robert E. Lee took command of the Army on June 1, he did not receive the Map of

BIRDS EYE VIEW
OF THE
SEAT OF WAR AROUND RICHMOND
SHOWING THE BATTLE ON CHICKAHOMINY RIVER

Julius Bachmann, Publisher

Henrico County until June 21, and he reportedly had the single Confederate map of the area! As mentioned in the foreword, this situation was so bad, it led Brigadier General Richard Taylor of Jackson's Valley Army (whose picture appears on p. 53) to comment:

"The Confederates knew no more about the topography of the country then they did about Central Africa. Here was a limited district, the whole of it within a day's march of the city of Richmond, capital of Virginia and the Confederacy, almost the first spot of the Continent occupied by the British race... and yet we were profoundly ignorant of the country, were without maps, sketches or proper guides, and nearly as helpless as if we had been transferred to the banks of the Lualaba [the Congo]."

The Confederates often had to rely on sketches in lieu of maps, such as Captain Blackford's map of the Union position at Harrison's Landing (p. 64).

The Civil War was also very difficult for the public to understand, with bloody battles in far-off places. Maps such as the "Seat of War in America" (p. 66) informed the American, and in this case, the British public about the location of events. At one point in the Peninsula Campaign, *Harper's Weekly* obtained a copy of A.A. Humphreys "Map of Yorktown." As the siege was still in progress, this could have aided the Confederates, which prompted a sharp rebuke from Captain Humphreys for publishing classified maps.

Powder smoke rises from the banks of the Chickahominy River in this imaginary but creative aerial perspective of the June 29, 1862 engagement at Glendale, one of the Seven Days battles in which Robert E. Lee's army forced McClellan's withdrawal from the environs of Richmond.

Chapter 5

The Antietam Campaign

*T*he war's bloodiest day, as Antietam came to be called, was the grim climax of a four-month campaign by Robert E. Lee in which the historical reputation of the North's "Little Napoleon," Major General George Brinton McClellan, was destroyed. Unfortunately for Lee and the South, outwitting Union generals was one thing; combating the Army of the Potomac would prove far more difficult.

At Antietam, or Sharpsburg as the South called it, the Union, despite McClellan, came closer to capturing Lee and the entire Army of Northern Virginia than it would for another three years.

But before he brushed disaster at Antietam, Lee conducted his most risky and perhaps his most brilliant battles. Starting with his defeat of McClellan's Peninsula Campaign against Richmond, a series of clashes produced another major battle at Manassas, or Bull Run: Lee, Longstreet, and Jackson defeated smaller Federal forces and then defeated the army of Major General John Pope, who had come from the successful river campaigns of the West.

Pope's Army of Virginia was organized in early June to pressure Lee from the North as McClellan approached Richmond from the East. But Pope got off to a bad start with his troops by praising the success of his Western army comrades. One of the most unintentionally apt remarks of the war was uttered by Pope when intending to inspire men he saw as effete Easterners he announced that henceforth, his "headquarters would be in the saddle."

The polite version of the immediate rejoinder was "Pope's head was where his hindquarters should be," and Pope's subsequent bungling against Lee confirmed to the skeptical soldiers that their gibes were well-founded.

Troop positions at the commencement of the battle of Antietam were plotted by William H. Willcox, a lieutenant of the 95th New York who served as topographical engineer on General Abner Doubleday's staff. Doubleday's division suffered heavy losses in the advance through Miller's cornfield.

Confederate dead lay sprawled beside an abandoned artillery limber near the Hagerstown Pike and Dunker Church (background), ground that changed hands several times in the day-long battle at Antietam.
LC B8184-40497

Despite uncharacteristically poor tactical judgment by Jackson at the Battle of Cedar Mountain, on August 9, and Longstreet on the first day of Second Manassas on the 29th, by August 30 Lee completed a month-long series of maneuvers as risky as anything he ever attempted: faced by numbers sometimes two or three times his available strength, Lee split his army into two and sometimes three smaller forces, defeating or driving off Federal armies.

Lee felt free to march north against Pope and the ill-coordinated Federal forces guarding Washington because he knew that since McClellan's grand army was leaving by boat, it couldn't reinforce Pope if the Confederates moved quickly. And Lee felt compelled by the knowledge that if Pope and McClellan ever joined forces, the Army of Northern Virginia and the Confederacy would likely be overwhelmed. A daring cavalry raid on Pope's headquarters by Fitzhugh Lee, the General's nephew, captured Pope's clothing, which was embarrassing, and his plans, which proved fatal. Lee now knew he could strike Pope before McClellan's army arrived.

By contrast, Pope, on the first day of Second Manassas, thought that he faced Jackson's isolated 20,000 troops, that Longstreet was nowhere near, and that Lee's army was retreating into the Shenandoah Valley. Pope had already missed a chance to smash Jackson and Longstreet separately, and his subordinate commanders, including McClellan's ally, Fitz John Porter, lost what little confidence in him they still had and openly criticized his plans and capacities. Lee, who had come to despise Pope, was now in position to humiliate his pompous rival.

In ignorance of his superiority, Pope wasted the morning in unsupported probing attacks by elements of his 62,000-man army. Longstreet finally came to Jackson's rescue shortly before noon, and had they combined to attack Pope, the Federals might have been routed a day sooner.

August 30 saw Pope's army handed a shattering tactical defeat when Lee used Longstreet's corps in a surprise flank attack. Only a desperate stand on the late Widow Henry's Hill, this time by the Union, allowed Pope's army to flee across the Stone Bridge over Bull Run, and back to Washington.

Keeping up the pressure, Lee pushed a flanking movement toward Fairfax Court House. The subsequent Battle of Chantilly on September 1 killed two of the Union's most promising commanders, Major Generals Phil Kearney and Isaac Stevens. Kearney, who lost an arm in the Mexican War, was an "Old Army" favorite of Lee's and of many Confederate officers, who sadly returned his body through the lines. Stevens had been under consideration to replace McClellan.

Lee had smashed Pope, but not his army. McClellan now arrived with the Army of the Potomac, and Lincoln realized that only McClellan had the trust of the soldiers for the coming crisis. The Army of Northern Virginia was rampaging about the Maryland countryside, headed for who knew where: Philadelphia, Washington, Baltimore.

For Lee had determined that even if he couldn't defeat the massive Union army in the field, he could make use of McClellan's characteristic caution for a quick raid into Maryland and Pennsylvania. This would take pressure off Richmond and offered untapped resources of supplies. Lee was also led to believe, falsely, that the army would attract thousands of eager recruits for the South. Some of Lee's best fighters were the Maryland regiments, and only Lincoln's strong-arm tactics at the outset of the war had held slave-state Maryland in the Union. Lee also hoped that a foray over the border would further demoralize the North, following the defeats of the summer, and such costly victories as Shiloh, and that the peace movement might gain strength against the Lincoln Administration.

Even from this distance, the risk Lee now embarked on is breathtaking. His men had been fighting since the beginning of the summer and had defeated both of the main Union armies in the East: they were out of food, clothing, shoes, indeed out of everything except ammunition, faith in themselves, and faith in Lee. But not all of them agreed with his decision to go North. Many men, including entire units, refused to cross into Maryland, arguing that they had volunteered to defend the South, not to invade another country. Reinforcements brought Lee's strength back up to 50,000 for the campaign.

Lee's strategy wasn't risky, but his tactics were: facing McClellan's combined army of more than 75,000 Lee deployed in a Napoleonic "fan," splitting Longstreet and Jackson for different assignments, and further subdividing his army throughout western Maryland. At first, it appeared if he would get away with it, as McClellan, with no idea of Lee's whereabouts or intentions, moved very carefully north and west, seeking the Rebels while reorganizing his own forces.

Screened by Stuart's cavalry, Lee split his forces after reaching Frederick, Maryland, sending Jackson to capture the Union armory and supplies at Harper's Ferry, across the Potomac in west Virginia. Longstreet went toward Hagerstown, Maryland, from where Lee planned to strike into Pennsylvania, to investigate reports of Union forces in the area.

Lee's Special Order 191, detailing the "fan," thus had five small detachments operating on different missions with the assumption that Stuart would warn him of McClellan's

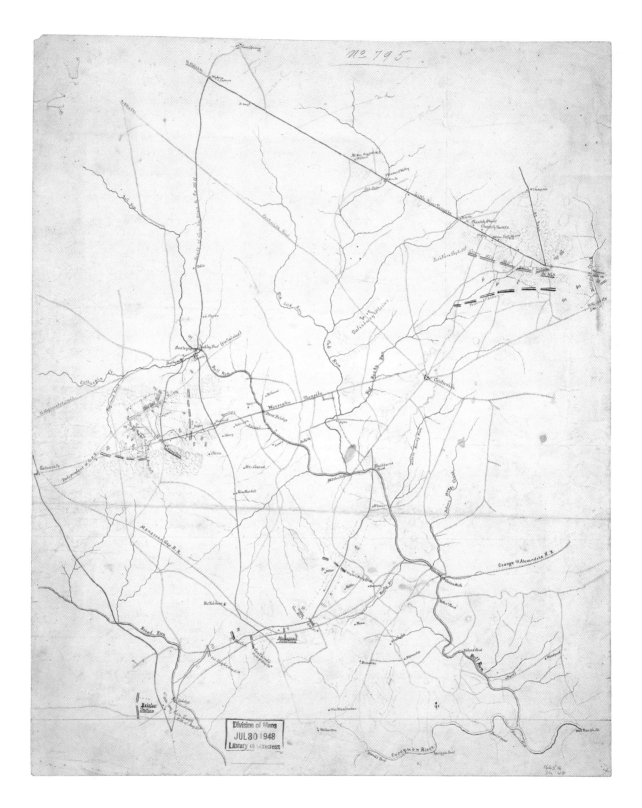

A January 1863 map by famed cartographer Jedediah Hotchkiss traces the route of Stonewall Jackson's corps in the latter stages of the Second Manassas campaign. On September 1, two days after the Confederate victory on the old battlefield of Bull Run, Jackson's men again clashed with elements of Pope's Federal army at Ox Hill (upper right).

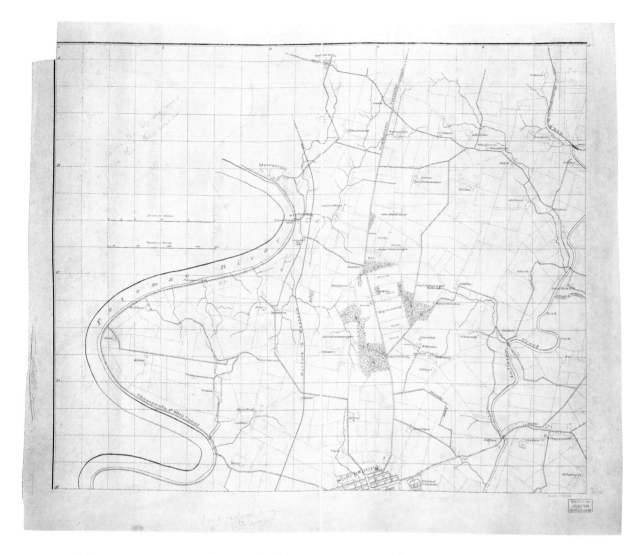

approach in time to reunite and escape back to Virginia. It might have worked, except for three cigars.

McClellan finally reached Frederick on September 13, and some tired footsoldiers seeking a rest found the cigars in a field, wrapped in a copy of Special Order 191 intended for A.P. Hill. "Here is a paper with which if I cannot whip Bobby Lee, I will be willing to go home," McClellan shouted. Orders were quickly dispatched uniting his army in a push to defeat Lee's scattered units.

Word soon reached Lee of McClellan's uncharacteristic haste, and his suspicions were confirmed when a civilian witness to McClellan's exultation reported the Federals' discovery. Longstreet was recalled to block South Mountain and delay McClellan; "Little Mac" meanwhile dispatched a corps to drive Jackson away from Harper's Ferry. Lee ordered his

A wartime map by Captain Nathaniel Michler, U.S. Corps of Engineers, was enlarged and revised in 1894 when the Antietam Battlefield Commission put forth plans to preserve the site as a park. The infamous "Bloody Lane," a sunken road once strewn with the bodies of Confederate soldiers, appears north of Sharpsburg and the National Cemetery.

army to attempt to unite around Sharpsburg, on Antietam Creek.

At Harper's Ferry, neither Jackson nor the 12,000 Union defenders knew of McClellan's luck and General William B. Franklin's rescue mission. Ordered by Washington to hold on at all costs, the pressure apparently collapsed the already shaky moral and mental faculties of Colonel Dixon Miles, the garrison's commander, who had been found drunk on the field at First Bull Run.

Even as Franklin's column drew near, Jackson's pressure broke Miles's will, and he decided to surrender on September 15. This outraged the Federal cavalry commanders in the garrison and they demanded permission to escape. Major Augustus Corliss told his Rhode Island troopers they were going to try to ride out at night through Jackson's encircling army and predicted "by tomorrow, you will be in Pennsylvania, on the way to Richmond, or in Hell!" He was two-thirds right: after their successful escape, the troops captured Longstreets ammunition wagons, took themto Greencastle, Pennsylvania, and headed for Antietam.

Jackson left A.P. Hill at Harper's Ferry to load the huge stock of captured arms and ammunition and sent word to Lee he was rushing to join him. Lee decided not to flee across the border to Virginia, but to consolidate the army at Sharpsburg and fight. He got the time to do this from the remarkable stand by Major General D.H. Hill's division of Longstreet's corps in the passes of South Mountain. Lee's confidence in McClellan's timidity, even with Order 191 in his possession, was confirmed.

By the afternoon of September 16, Lee and 19,000 men sat with their backs to the Potomac while McClellan approached with 70,000 Federals. The trouble, of course, was that McClellan didn't think he faced so few, and wouldn't have believed it if told. As he had throughout the Peninsula Campaign, McClellan continued to rely on the estimates of his Chief of Intelligence, the railroad detective Allan Pinkerton. Pinkerton, as on the Peninsula, gave McClellan highly inflated estimates of Lee's strength. McClellan arrived on the hills overlooking Sharpsburg thinking he would have to fight 200,000 Confederates.

McClellan also was up against something he couldn't control, and that was the myth of invincibility that Lee and his army had built since the previous June. The Army of Northern Virginia by Antietam had developed a moral force that affected all who saw it. Jackson's capture of Harper's Ferry left this indelible impression on a Union infantry officer: "It was a weird and uncanny sight, and drove sleep from my eyes. They were silent as ghosts; ruthless and rushing in their speed; ragged, earth-colored, dishevelled and devilish, as though keen on the scent of hot blood. Their sliding dog-trot was as though on snow-shoes. The shuffle of their badly shod feet on the hard surface of the pike was so rapid as to be continuous like the hiss of a great serpent. The spectral picture will never be effaced from my memory."

Lee had posted his indeed-filthy army in a strong defensive position across a ridge north of Sharpsburg, which would force the Federals to attack uphill while his artillery fired down on them. McClellan, instead of immediately testing Lee's strength, did what Lee had anticipated: he delayed to plan the perfect battle. This took a full 24 hours, allowing all but A.P. Hill's division of Jackson's corps to join the Army of Northern Virginia, which now numbered 40,000, still less than half of the Army of the Potomac.

McClellan planned to attack at dawn on the 17th, in three separate grand assaults, the

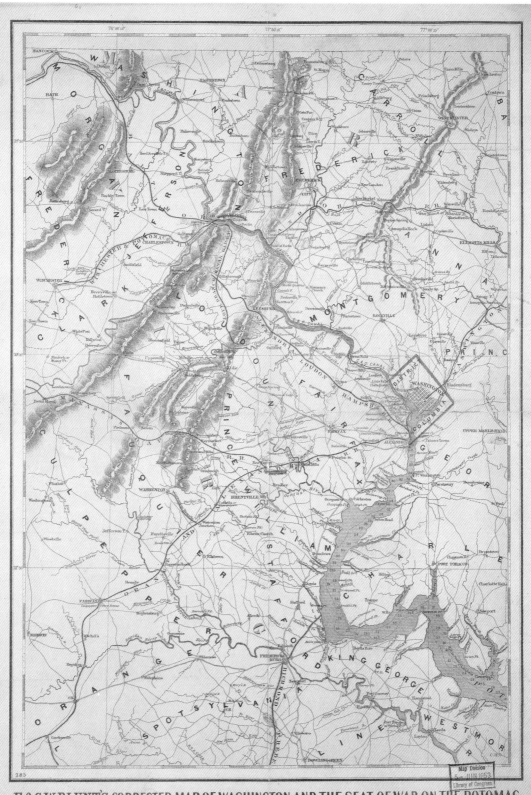

E&G.W.BLUNT'S CORRECTED MAP OF WASHINGTON AND THE SEAT OF WAR ON THE POTOMAC.

This map of the "Seat of War on the Potomac" plainly features the Blue Ridge
and Bull Run Mountain ranges: natural barriers which Robert E. Lee used to
screen his army's advance against General John Pope's forces in August, 1862.

On the moonlit night of September 4, 1862, Union pickets open fire on the vanguard of Lee's forces as they wade across the Potomac River from Virginia into Maryland. White's Ford was a favorite crossing point for both armies, its environs the scene of numerous skirmishes.

main and first one coming on the left of Lee's thin line, the north flank, followed by pushes on the right, toward Harper's Ferry, and then up the center. If any of the attacks seemed to be working, McClellan would then commit his reserves and sweep Lee from the field.

Such piecemeal attacks allowed Lee to shift his forces on interior lines to whatever point was threatened. McClellan's last-minute reorganization of the army into sectors with new overall commanders might have worked had McClellan made each general aware of his part in the whole; instead, McClellan kept his basic plan to himself, and kept all coordination and communication control in his own hands. The inevitable result was that his fighting arms knew nothing except what was before them.

The attack was to be led on the right by the ambitious, vain, and perhaps disloyal (to McClellan) Joseph Hooker, for all of that a strong fighter. But Hooker's First Corps made such a racket getting into place the night before that Lee was confident in predicting the main attack in the morning, and shifted his forces accordingly. During the night, McClellan moved General Joseph Mansfield's Twelfth Corps into support behind Hooker, with General Edwin Sumner's Second Corps behind them.

Facing Hooker across 400 yards of farmer David Miller's cornfield were Stonewall Jackson and his 7,700 men, about 1,000 fewer than Hooker's force. Jackson's artillery was supplemented by Jeb Stuart's Horse Artillery, under John Pelham. The attack began with Hooker's men making good progress until the guns opened up, and in minutes all of the corn was down, scythed close to the ground, survivors reported, along with hundreds of Union soldiers. Thus began a series of fifteen charges and countercharges, a holocaust that destroyed entire regiments on both sides, famous units like the Louisiana Tigers, and green regiments in their first battle.

Just as Jackson's men wavered General John Bell Hood's Texans broke the First Corp's push, but when Hood got back to his lines, he reported his division "dead on the field." They had run headlong into Mansfield's Corps. The white-bearded Mansfield had hoped to crown a forty-year army career with a triumph in battle, but a sharpshooter mortally wounded him before he came in sight of Hood. With Mansfield down, and Hooker painfully wounded and off the field, McClellan's hoped-for main attack lost momentum. It was 9 in the morning, and already 8,000 men on both sides had been shot.

McClellan had been watching all of this through a spyglass from his headquarters hill across Antietam Creek. Lee, by contrast, had been up in the front lines, and so absorbed in the fighting that at one point his artillerist son, Robert Jr., had to introduce himself. Finally, McClellan ordered in his reserves for the main assault, Sumner's Second Corps. Complicating Sumner's task was the continued failure of General Ambrose Burnside to launch his long-overdue diversionary attack on the Confederate right flank.

"Bull" Sumner hurt himself by charging through the woods without asking for intelligence of what lay in his front. Two hours of fighting killed or wounded nearly half of Sumner's force up by the Dunker Church, near the cornfield. Still without instructions from McClellan, Sumner and his men shifted the focus of the battle to Lee's center, weakly defended by only D.H. Hill's division of Longstreet's corps. However, two brigades occupied a very strong position, a winding path on top of a ridge that became known as Bloody Lane. In a virtual repeat of the cornfield fight, Federal troops finally gained a foothold from which to drive the Rebels from the field, but no support was sent, and the opportunity was lost.

The same thing happened to the other point of Lee's center which came to have a simple name capitalized by history, the Sunken Road. Again the Federals got a foothold that could have routed Lee, but no support came. Longstreet's staff personally manned artillery that smashed the Yankees as D.H. Hill counterattacked. The Federal area commander, Israel Richardson, was mortally wounded by a canister shot, and this stopped the Federal momentum. Longstreet later reported, "We were already badly whipped, and only holding our ground by sheer force of desperation."

But desperation was enough, as McClellan missed his and the Union's single great opportunity in the war to end it in a moment: despite his plans he held back his strike force, Fitz John Porter's Fifth Corps, throughout the battle. Even so, McClellan still might have won save for Ambrose Burnside.

The Stone House at the intersection of the Warrenton Turnpike and Sudley Road had witnessed heavy fighting during the first battle at Bull Run. A year later, General John Pope's Union army was soundly thrashed by Robert E. Lee's Confederates on the same ground, and the blood of wounded soldiers again stained the home's floors.
LC B8184-4227

Burnside, as unlucky a man and commander as any in the history of the Army of the Potomac, had been ordered by McClellan to attack across Antietam Creek to divert Lee from Hooker's attack. But Burnside spent the night resting, rather than preparing. He didn't know that his 11,000 man Ninth Corps, with 50 cannon, was opposing all of 550 Confederates, for General Robert Toombs' Rebels were well posted, and their rifle and artillery fire was focused to block access to the narrow stone bridge across the creek. And in truth, Burnside was sulking, angry because his old friend, McClellan, had been short with him of late, and on the eve of battle had removed him from the joint command of the Ninth and First Corps.

The Federals finally struggled across what would be called Burnside's Bridge shortly after 1 p.m., just as the Union drive to Bloody Lane, in the center, was stalling. So by default, Burnside's diversion was to become McClellan's last great effort to break Lee's lines. After delays to bring up ammunition the attack started well, but the lull allowed Lee and Longstreet to shift artillery to the hills overlooking Burnside's men, while the Confederates prayed for A.P. Hill to arrive from Harper's Ferry.

At 2 p.m., Hill's advance units came within sight of the field, and Hill, in his flaming-red battle shirt, galloped ahead to be embraced by Lee. Burnside's plan was to drive right up to Sharpsburg itself. The advance made it to within 200 yards of town, but the corps was strung out and vulnerable just as Hill's division completed its seventeen-mile, eight-hour forced march.

Hill's 3,000 men slammed into the attenuated Federal flanks as though it had all been perfectly planned. Isaac Rodman was killed, the ninth Union general to be shot that day. Up on the Confederate lines, one of Hill's brigadiers, Lawrence Branch, was shot down as he raised binoculars to watch the Federal situation. He was the ninth Confederate general to fall.

It was now late afternoon, and had McClellan even then made one big attack, he could have won. With A.P. Hill, Lee had played his last card, while McClellan had just been reinforced. He had Porter and more than 10,000 fresh troops to throw at Lee's exhausted men. But McClellan had spent the day fearing a Confederate counterattack by the 200,000 men Pinkerton had reported, and at this last, great chance he couldn't risk defeat.

Lee defiantly stayed all the next day, September 18, before withdrawing his battered army when it became obvious McClellan wasn't going to move. After all that, it was a tactical draw, although McClellan could legitimately claim that for the first time, Robert E. Lee had left a field without winning, and the Confederate invasion had been turned back.

Strategically, Antietam was made into a victory by the Lincoln Administration, which badly needed a success in the East after a summer of failure. Lincoln took Antietam as the leverage needed to issue the Emancipation Proclamation, giving the Confederacy a strategic defeat on a worldwide scale. The British government, which had been seriously contemplating recognizing Southern independence, now felt it had better wait for clearer signs to the future of the Union. They came, but not until the summer of 1863, at Vicksburg and Gettysburg.

Antietam was called the bloodiest day of the war, correctly: one of every four men became casualties. Of the 75,000 Union troops in the battle, more than 12,400 fell, with 2,108 killed outright, 9,549 wounded and hundreds dead later as a result of wounds or injury. Of

Lee's estimated 45,000 men, at least 1,546 were killed, 7,752 were wounded, and 1,018 were reported missing, many actually dead.

The nineteenth general officer to become a casualty of Antietam was McClellan. Lincoln finally became so exasperated by Little Mac's inability to destroy the Army of Northern Virginia that he removed McClellan on November 5, almost two years from the day that he would defeat him at the polls in the election of 1864.

While McClellan was a poor map officer, Irvin McDowell (pictured on p. 22) was a good one. His First Corps was stationed in Northern Virginia from the fall of 1861 through the late summer of 1862, and his Topographical Engineer, Captain Whipple, put this time to good use by surveying and compiling a good map of the area. This "McDowell Map" was used by many of the commanders of John Pope's ill-fated Army of Virginia during the campaign of Second Manassas.

The Bureau of Topographic Engineers in Washington was still unable to meet the huge demand for maps, and commanders were forced to turn to commercial copies, such as the Blunt map (p. 81). During the Second Manassas Campaign, in July of 1862, the Topographic Bureau answered a map request from Franz Sigel, Corps Commander:

"Sir, we have no photographic copies of the nine sheet map [1859 Buchholtz] of Va. We had a few copies of the four sheet map [1824 original Boye], but these are exhausted. The map of Va. published by Lloyd is quite good if not better than the four sheet map, and can be procured at the book stores for twenty five cents each."

Antietam was the first Confederate invasion of the North, and the Confederates seemed to have had adequate knowledge of the area. Although it was not until November 1862 that Robert E. Lee was given a complete lithographed map of the "Seat of War" in the East, the Confederates reported no mapping difficulties during the Antietam Campaign. In fact, the Confederates seemed to have known the locations of the Potomac River fords and the roads as well as the Union troops did. This may have been due to the large towns in the area, such as Leesburg, Frederick, and Harpers Ferry and the well-traveled East-West routes such as the 18th Century National Road, the C&O Canal, and the B&O Railroad. It certainly helped to have good topographers such as Hotchkiss (Second Manassas Map, p.78). The U.S. government also recognized his talent, and after the War, he was hired to draw battlefield park maps, such as the 1894 Antietam map of Nathaniel Michler (p.79).

Union telegraphers hastily string an improvised line of communication during the December 13, 1862 battle of Fredericksburg.
LC USZ62-1057

Chapter 6

The Vicksburg Campaign

U.S. Grant hated, indeed refused to retrace his steps exactly. Once he realized he was on the wrong path, he preferred some entirely new route to simply going back to the start and trying again. That, in a nutshell, describes the Vicksburg Campaign: Sam Grant just keeping at it until he found a way to break into the city high on the bluffs of the Mississippi River, and so break the Confederacy in two.

The Union's campaign against Vicksburg actually began in the summer of 1862. Shortly after Grant's victory at Shiloh, a combined army-navy operation under Admiral David G. Farragut moved against a virtually unguarded Vicksburg to follow up Farragut's earlier capture of New Orleans.

But in a taste of what was to come, Vicksburg's small garrison was able to drive away Farragut's fleet with considerable damage, and even more embarrassment to the Hero of New Orleans. A preview of what was in store for Federal ground forces came in the form of a prodigious effort by General Thomas Williams's brigade to dig a canal through the narrow peninsula across from the city. But the army abandoned its digging on July 26, the same day the navy admitted defeat and steamed downriver to New Orleans and the Gulf of Mexico, where they would be free of Rebel sharpshooters and plunging fire from shore batteries.

So it wasn't until the fall of 1862, after Henry Halleck replaced George McClellan as General-in-Chief in Washington, that Federal commanders began to contemplate another crack at Vicksburg. On October 25, almost by default, Grant became Commander of the Department of the Tennessee when Halleck couldn't come up with anyone else for the job. Following Grant's embarrassment on

This map of the Confederate defenses of Vicksburg was based on reconnaissances made by Clarence Fendall, a civilian employee of the U.S. Coast Survey serving with Admiral David D. Porter's Mississippi River squadron.

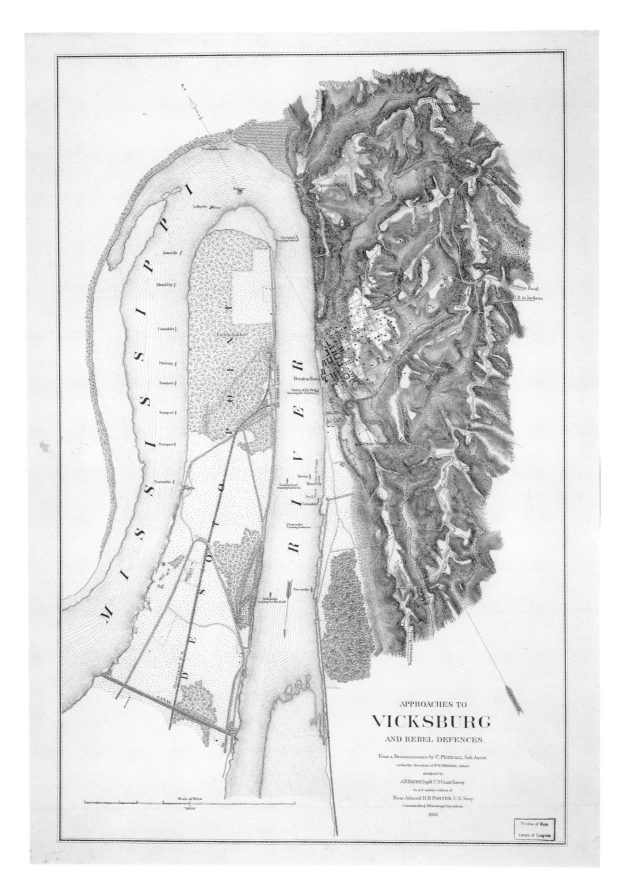

APPROACHES TO
VICKSBURG
AND REBEL DEFENCES.

From a Reconnaissance by C. PENDALL, Sub Assist.
under the direction of F.H. GERDES, Assist.
assigned by
A.D.BACHE, Supdt. U.S Coast Survey
to act under orders of
Rear Admiral D.D.PORTER, U.S.Navy
Commanding Mississippi Squadron.
1863.

Scale of Miles

Bombproof shelters constructed by the 45th Illinois of General John A. Logan's division honeycombe a hillside near Vicksburg, Mississippi. The white Shirley house was used as Logan's headquarters.
LC USZ62-11875

Shiloh's first day, rumors of his drinking problems, and Halleck's jealousy of Grant's fame once again nearly cost the Union the services of the man who eventually led it to victory.

But one week after assuming command in the West, Grant started what was to be the most imaginative and successful military movement of the war, the Vicksburg Campaign.

Grant's first plan was the simplest: a fast, hard push from the Tennessee border straight down the Mississippi Central Railroad to the capital, Jackson, and then a sharp western dash along the railroad linking Jackson to Vicksburg. He didn't expect much opposition, and felt that Vicksburg might well surrender at his approach. Politics and hard-driving Confederate cavalry relieved Grant of his illusions.

Political reality came from Grant's rival, Major General John McClernand, who persuaded Lincoln to allow him to recruit an army of Western men for a river-borne attack on Vicksburg. Although ambitious, McClernand was a patriotic man and his plan had merit. But Grant, whose reputation as a political naif stemmed from his later failures as President, quickly determined that if Lincoln favored a waterborne Vicksburg effort, he would have one of Grant's devising, not McClernand's.

President Davis and the Richmond authorities were fully aware of Grant's general designs, of course; Davis owned a plantation just below Vicksburg, and in December Davis and General Joseph

Johnston visited the city. The Southern president had already replaced the reckless Earl Van Dorn at Vickburg with a Pennsylvanian loyal to his wife's South, Lieutenant General John Pemberton. Van Dorn returned to his forté, the cavalry, and swiftly gave Grant an unwelcome Christmas present in the form of the destruction of the massive Federal supply depot at Holly Springs, Mississippi.

A simultaneous raid by Nathan Bedford Forrest's troopers broke up sixty miles of railroad north of Jackson, the two Southern cavalrymen thus effectively breaking Grant's planned overland route almost before the journey got started. Unfortunately for the South, while Davis and Johnston had stressed Vickburg's importance, they had not reached a consensus on how to defend it. Davis and Pemberton felt the city should be held at all costs; Johnston favored keeping the army intact, even at the expense of territory (a debate still being waged between Davis and Johnston when Sherman reached the gates of Atlanta, in 1864). At Vicksburg, the consequences were ultimately fatal to Confederate hopes.

With the overland route proving to be not so simple, Grant determined to pursue the water route, secure in the knowledge that Lincoln personally favored the idea. Thus began the Bayou Expeditions, five ingenious but unsuccessful attempts by Grant and the navy to circumvent Vicksburg through tributaries and waterways parallel to the Mississippi. Grant himself called the attempts "experiments," although he had hopes that one of them would succeed.

All of these expeditions were made in heavy rains and high waters, but Grant felt that it was better to keep up morale by doing something, than to allow his army to get rusty in camp waiting for the spring. Sherman's corps took to enlarging the 1862 canal across from the city, but after enormous labors, it and a similar effort at Duckport, twenty miles below Vicksburg, proved useless.

The final bayou "experiment" was a 200-mile effort by Admiral Porter and his gunboats, supported by Sherman, up Steele's Bayou. Porter managed to get his eleven ships completely stuck far up into the swamps near Rolling Fork, at which point a frantic message reached Sherman on March 19: "Dear Sherman, hurry up, for Heaven's sake!" A night march by 10,000 Federal soldiers, many with candles in their muskets, reached Porter the next day and disaster was averted.

In time Grant's various attempts up to this point were seen as an interesting part of the whole, and proof of his tenacious character. But in March, 1863, all the country could see was weeks of failure, and no success in sight. Coming on the heels of George McClellan's incomplete victory at Antietam in September, and the true disaster at Fredericksburg in December, the only recent success the Lincoln Administration could point to was the costly draw at Stones River, Tennessee, December 31-January 2.

The politically astute Grant recognized that if he gave up the waterborne attempts at Vicksburg to try again by the original land route, he would have to go all the way up to Memphis and start from scratch. Grant knew that the Northern press and people would see this as a retreat, and a Southern victory, one that might cost him his command. (In fact, Pemberton wired Richmond on April 11 that it looked as though Grant was giving up.) Instead, Grant took a course that helped define him: he took his army to the Vicksburg side of the river, completely cut off from his base of supplies, and attacked the city from the rear, as originally planned.

Union General John A. McClernand appended what he termed "a hasty sketch" of the approaches to Vicksburg in his February 14, 1863 report to President Lincoln. McClernand led an expedition which resulted in the capture of Arkansas Post (upper left).

Ever since Farragut's bloody efforts at running the Vicksburg batteries in July 1862, the navy had been wary of its ability to pass by, particularly with loaded troop transports as Grant's new plan would require. But on April 16, 1863, after preliminary rushes by isolated ships proved it could be done, Admiral Porter's main fleet and transports ran by at night.

To give himself time to consolidate before Pemberton's garrison and other Southern forces could concentrate against him, Grant ordered two showy diversions to mask his main thrust: the first was entrusted to Sherman, with ten regiments, who were to join with navy gunboats in a feint on Chickasaw Bluffs, the site of an embarrassment for Sherman in December. The new assignment went perfectly, and Pemberton diverted forces from Grant's beachhead to meet what his subordinates were convinced was the real attack.

The second diversion became one of the war's most celebrated cavalry exploits and, indeed, one of the few really successful cavalry raids of the war. Despite their dash and color, most cavalry expeditions before and after what became known as Grierson's Raid cost more in lost horses and men than was justified by lasting damage to the enemy. But on April 16, Colonel Benjamin H. Grierson, a music teacher and very reluctant horse soldier, led 1,700 troopers from three regiments on a remarkable 600-mile foray through the length of Mississippi and Louisiana.

Grierson's route drew the Confederates down and away from Grant's army, and diverted Confederate cavalry that otherwise would have been scouting and harassing Grant at his most vulnerable point. Starting from the Tennessee border, in sixteen days Grierson emerged at Baton Rouge, Louisiana, to the consternation of the Confederacy and the amazement of Federal occupation forces, which had been holed up waiting for some success by Grant or General Nathaniel Banks's Port Hudson expedition.

Grant's first attempt at a beachhead on the eastern shore, below Vicksburg, failed as Confederate shore batteries at Grand Gulf proved fatally accurate against several of Porter's ships. Acting on advice from a freed slave, Grant and Porter slipped ten miles further downriver and landed unopposed at Bruinsburg. The next day April 30, McClernand's Corps joined Grant, and the Federals for the first time had men and supplies on the ground, south and near to Vicksburg on the eastern bank of the Mississippi.

But Pemberton also moved quickly, and troops were sent down from Grand Gulf for a bitter fight on May l, around Port Gibson. The rugged and swampy country was ideal for defense, and Grant's 20,000 troops had a hard time dislodging 5,000 determined Confederates under General John Bowen, a West Point classmate of Grant's protegé, McPherson. Ultimately, the simultaneous diversions of Sherman and Grierson confused Pemberton to the point where he recalled all his forces to concentrate at Vicksburg. The Confederates thus lost their best chance to crush Grant before he had consolidated his position.

Grant's movements soon forced Bowen to abandon Grand Gulf itself on May 7. Despite his designs on Vicksburg, Grant initially planned to send a corps south to help Banks at Port Hudson, like Vicksburg a heavily fortified river fortress. This would open a supply line to New Orleans and allow a massive joint operation against Vicksburg. But Banks characteristically missed the opportunity by brushing aside Grant's plan and launching the first "Red River Expedition," seen by many as a cotton speculator's foraging party designed to enrich New England and New York merchants who had been suffering since 1861.

Grant thus made the decision that placed him in the front rank of history's military commanders: concluding that he couldn't wait for Banks, who in any event was senior and would have superseded him in a joint operation, Grant explained "I therefore determined to move independently of Banks, cut loose from my base, destroy the rebel force in the rear of Vicksburg and invest or capture the city." Basically, Grant resolved to turn military thinking on its head, and feed a large army off the enemy's land, in the face of a foe that at that point still outnumbered him.

Grant suspected that Halleck, Stanton, and possibly the president would never sustain this deviation from textbook maxims, but knew that by the time Washington heard about it, he would be on his way and beyond recall.

While Washington was kept happily ignorant, Pemberton quickly divined Grant's intentions and pleaded for help from Joe Johnston, help that Johnston opposed, then promised, and in the end failed to deliver. The gap between Johnston's notion that troops were more important than territory to the Confederacy, and Davis's conservative view that Vicksburg had to be held, caught Pemberton in a dilemma he could not resolve.

Grant had no such dilemma: he knew he had to strike at Jackson, Mississippi, quickly to stop a concentration of reinforcements for Vicksburg, and on May 12, his 44,000 men started to march. Grant's three wings, under Sherman, McPherson, and McClernand, brushed aside Southern units and reached Jackson in two days, just a day later, in fact, than a badly ailing Joe Johnston.

Johnston, still suffering from the severe wounds received nearly a year before in Virginia, found only 6,000 Confederates actually in place to resist Grant. He immediately informed Richmond "I am too late," and stopped any attempts at reinforcing the state capital. Although Sherman and McPherson's attacks in a driving rainstorm on May 14 were not well coordinated, the Federals soon broke the vastly outnumbered Confederates.

That night, Grant slept in the bed just occupied by Johnston, and a Union spy intercepted Johnston's orders to Pemberton, urging a joint attack on Sherman's exposed flank. Confident that knowledge of his foes' plans would help defeat them, Grant sent Johnston's message on to Vicksburg.

But it did not stir Pemberton to action. President Davis's earlier wishes kept him in Vicksburg, where he vacillated over a plan to drive south and cut Grant's communications. Finally Pemberton reluctantly acceded to Johnston's new orders: come north and strike Grant's rear before he reaches Vicksburg. The two armies met on May 16, 1863. Pemberton took two-thirds of his garrison, some 22,000 men, and hastily assumed a superior defensive position at Champion's Hill, overlooking the Jackson-Vicksburg road. McPherson and McClernand's 29,000 men were under the direct command of Grant, who had hurried over from Jackson, leaving Sherman's corps to burn everything of military value.

The first real battle Grant had directed since Shiloh, the year before, was bitterly fought but poorly coordinated by the Confederates. Pemberton chose an excellent position for the center of the line. But for reasons never fully explained, his flanks, held by Loring and Bowen, refused to concentrate and save the center until it was too late. Thus, despite very slow action by McClernand, hard fighting by McPherson's men and those of the dynamic politician, John "Black Jack" Logan broke Pemberton's lines.

In the Confederate retreat, Loring's 6,000 men were cut off, ended up retiring toward Jackson, and were lost to Vicksburg's defenders. The two armies had about the same numbers as those engaged at First Manassas, and each suffered about the same casualties: 410 Union killed, 1,844 wounded, while the Confederates reported 381 killed and approximately 1,800 wounded.

As a demoralized Confederate army filed back into Vicksburg, a thrilled Sherman and Grant raced ahead of their troops to gaze at the city. Sherman turned to Grant and frankly admitted that up to that point, he had doubted the wisdom of Grant's strategy.

But Vicksburg hadn't fallen yet, and Pemberton was delighted to

Charles W. Reed, who received the Medal of Honor for gallantry at Gettysburg, made this study of his imperturbable commander, U.S. Grant. One Union officer thought Grant "habitually wears an expression as if he had determined to drive his head through a brick wall, and was about to do it."

Federal troops man one of hundreds of siege batteries that surrounded the Rebel stronghold of Vicksburg. By mid-June 1863, some 200 Union guns were bombarding the beleaguered city, while Admiral Porter's gunboats fired an estimated 22,000 shells at the stubborn defenders.
LC B816-8181

discover that a good night's rest, plus reinforcement from the 10,000 fresh troops he had left behind, gave the defenders new hope as they filed into the formidable defense system of trenches constructed in a seven-mile arc behind the city. Grant, thinking he had but to walk into Vicksburg, received a rude shock when a general assault along the lines was easily thrown back onMay 19.

Grant tried again on the 22nd, this time with a huge artillery barrage for one hour before the attack. Pemberton's lines held. McClernand, on the left, said his troops were making headway and that one more assault would break into the city. Grant didn't believe it, but ordered the attack anyway. Hundreds of Federal lives were wasted, and Grant later said he regretted the attack as much as the tragic second assault at Cold Harbor, in 1864. McClernand was later relieved for bragging about his "great victory." This day, Grant's army suffered 3,199 casualties, including 502 killed in action.

Grant and Pemberton seemed to recognize a stalemate, and each side settled into a siege. Joe Johnston had earlier sent wise counsel against getting trapped, but sent no troops to help Pemberton break out. Grant soon assembled 71,000 men, so that he could keep

Johnston away while Vicksburg's defenders starved. The siege went on through June.

Both sides knew that unless Confederate help arrived, surrender was inevitable. On July 3, Pemberton concluded that further suffering by his troops and the people of Vicksburg was senseless, and asked Grant for terms. As he had now set into policy, Grant demanded unconditional surrender. He set the surrender for July 4, recognizing what a message of hope it would send throughout the Union on that anniversary. Johnston, who had finally decided to try and relieve Vicksburg, called off an attack he had scheduled for July 7.

Down river at Port Hudson the trapped defenders recognized that without Vicksburg they, too, were doomed, and so surrendered to Banks on July 9. The Mississippi was now under Federal control; the campaigns that had begun at Forts Henry and Donelson more than a year previously had worked, largely because a modest and simple man, possessed of personal strength and political wisdom, simply refused to admit defeat.

The significance of Grant's victory was immediate and obvious. A jubilant Lincoln said "Now the Father of Waters again flows unvexed to the sea." Coming on the heels of Gettysburg, this split the Confederacy in two, and Grant was now firmly on the path of public and political support that would ultimately end the war.

On April 30, when Grant landed his Army at Bruinsburg on the Vicksburg side of the Mississippi, he was really entering a black hole of information, but at least he was on the same side of the river as his enemy. Vicksburg was such a "tough nut to crack" because it was situated on 100-foot bluffs overlooking a bend in the river (p. 87). Admiral Porter ran his gunboats under these bluffs to support Grant's landing (pp. 90-91).

Grant had a general idea of where the towns, such as Port Gibson, Grand Gulf, and Jackson were, but he had little knowledge of roads or rivers, such as the Bayou Pierre and the Big Black. He simply collected the information as he went along, often receiving it from freed slaves. On May 1, his little army ran into a strong Confederate position outside Port Gibson, established by Confederate General Bowen. Bowen had weakened Grand Gulf to try and prevent Grant's army from heading north. Bowen's better knowledge of the terrain allowed him to choose a wooded ridge as his good defense position, but Grant's superior numbers decided the issue. The second opportunity Grant could have exploited with better maps occurred during the Battle of Champion Hill on May 16. At a key moment of the battle, General John Logan (whose Vicksburg Headquarters are shown on p. 88), discovered that Confederate General Pemberton's left was "in the air," and could be easily turned. At that point, however, Logan had already been ordered to support the costly assault against the center of the Confederate line. The North was still victorious, but they missed an opportunity to severely damage Pemberton's defenders before they retreated into the Citadel of Vicksburg, a chance they might have used if they had had an adequate map of the hill.

Generals frequently used maps in a political fashion with their official reports, and General McClernand was one of the most political of generals. He had led an expedition to take Arkansas Post in February of 1863, with an army he named the Army of the Mississippi, clearly dreaming of bigger prizes. After capturing the post, he reportedly exclaimed: "Glorious! Glorious! My star is ever in the ascendant... I'll make a splendid report!" Grant was aware of his political ambitions, and frankly, did not trust him. During the assault on Vicksburg, his pride led to the second assault on the city (p. 95), for which Grant ultimately had him relieved with the statement:

"General McClernand's dispatches misled me as to the real state of facts, and caused much of this loss. He is entirely unfit for the position of corps commander, both on the march and on the battlefield."

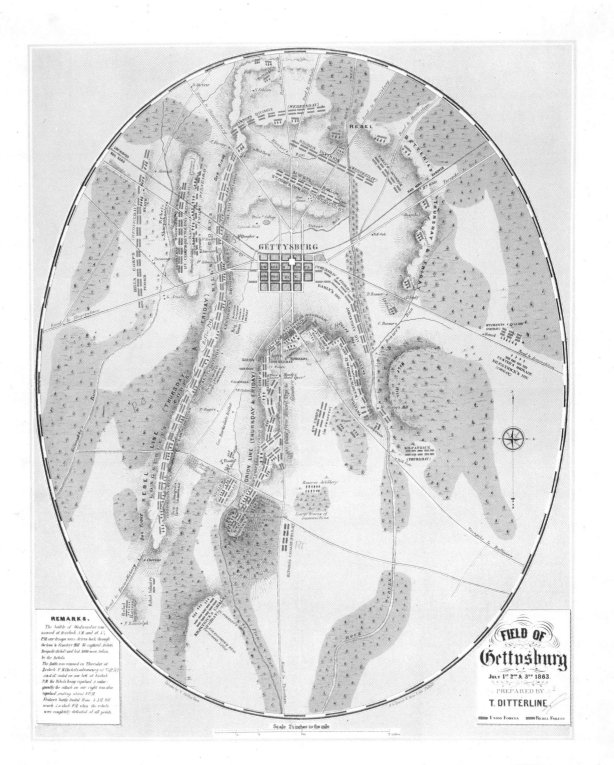

FIELD OF
Gettysburg
JULY 1ST 2ND & 3RD 1863.
PREPARED BY
T. DITTERLINE.

REMARKS.

The battle of Wednesday commenced at 10 o'clock A.M. and at 1½ P.M. our troops were driven back through the town to Cemetery Hill. We captured Archer's Brigade (Rebel) and lost 3000 men taken by the Rebels.

The battle was renewed on Thursday at 3 o'clock P.M. Sickels advancing at 5½P.M) and it ended on our left at 8 o'clock P.M. the Rebels being repulsed. Consequently the attack on our right was also repulsed ending about 8 P.M.

Friday's battle lasted from 4 A.M. till about 5 o'clock P.M. when the rebels were completely defeated at all points.

Scale 2½ inches to the mile

Chapter 7

Gettysburg

*T*he most important battle in American history began in a welter of confusion and consternation for the North, and in hope, anticipation and confidence for the South.

Thanks to a combination of daring and Union bungling that still seems incredible some 130 years later, Robert E. Lee and Stonewall Jackson combined to humiliate Joseph Hooker's Army of the Potomac, twice its size, in May. The swirling battles around Chancellorsville, in the "Wilderness" west of Fredericksburg, Virginia and out toward Culpeper, thwarted a well-planned Union thrust at Lee's Army of Northern Virginia.

Even as Hooker drew his frustrated army back toward the nation's capital, Lee and his lieutenants decided upon another of the bold, offensive raids into the North that had led to the strategic loss at Antietam the previous September. Stonewall Jackson had played a critical role in saving Lee at Antietam, but while Jackson's flank attack had routed the Union's Eleventh Corps at Chancellorsville, he and members of his staff were shot down by Confederate troops firing into the night at unknown horsemen.

Lee's famous and prophetic letter to a dying Jackson, "You have lost your left arm, but I have lost my right," foreshadowed the Confederate's tragedy-to-come in the sleepy Pennsylvania farm country. But in retrospect, Lee's troubles began to multiply well before the measure of Jackson's loss was taken at Gettysburg. Historians have rightly made much of the strategic error Lee committed in giving open-ended orders to the army's "eyes and ears," Jeb Stuart and his 10,000 cavalry.

John Singleton Mosby, not yet the "Gray Ghost," reported to Stuart that his mass of horsemen could slip through Hooker's lines south and west of Washington by a route that was closed by the time Stuart got

When Theodore Ditterline published an 1863 pamphlet entitled "Sketch of the battles of Gettysburg," he included this oval-shaped map of the three-day engagement. The famous "fish-hook" line held by General Meade's army on the second and third days of the battle is clearly visible at center.

In April, 1863 Captain George Armstrong Custer (left) strikes a typically jaunty pose with his commanding officer, Brigadier General Alfred Pleasonton. On June 29, the 23-year-old Custer was one of three young captains Pleasonton jumped to Brigadier General — part of his efforts to revitalize the Army of the Potomac's cavalry arm.
LC B8171-7551

going. The resulting loss of 24 to 36 hours proved to be the difference between Stuart's performing his proper function in the campaign, and his dramatic failure.

Joe Hooker's wounded ego caused him to pierce the limits of President Lincoln's patience with an ill-timed resignation as he started to pursue Lee through Maryland, toward Pennsylvania. To Hooker's and Lee's consternation, the new commander of the Army of the Potomac became the reliable, if less imaginative, George Meade. Lee remembered his new opponent from the "Old Army." The appointment was a surprise, as Meade was neither colorful nor well known.

For the first time, Lee and the Confederacy were facing an Army of the Potomac led at nearly all levels by men who were battle tested, determined, and free of the illusions or delusions that had so crippled George McClellan, John Pope, and Joe Hooker.

Meade took command on June 28 and found himself moving his seven-corps, 70,000-man army up the center of western Maryland through Frederick toward Pennsylvania. Meade thus split Jeb Stuart completely from Lee's army, as Stuart was glory hunting to avenge his embarrassing surprise by Union cavalry in the June 9 battle of Brandy Station. The Rebel troopers chased Union supply wagons toward Baltimore, before swinging northwest with their booty in a blind search for Lee.

But the 60,000-strong Army of Northern Virginia was far away, shielded by the Blue Ridge Mountains passing through the old Antietam battlefield at Sharpsburg and heading on through Maryland toward Chambersburg, Pennsylvania. From there, Richard Ewell, "Old Bald Head" to his men, foraged on up through Carlisle, threatening Harrisburg, the state capital, before sliding in the direction of Gettysburg, to the south.

Lee's other corps commanders, A.P. Hill and James Longstreet, also found themselves moving east from Chambersburg toward Gettysburg, after one of Longstreet's scouts, traditionally an actor named Harrison, accurately reported to Lee what Stuart could not: the whereabouts and intentions of the Union Army.

Historians have made much of the fact that the Confederates were seeking stocks of shoes rumored to be in Gettysburg, a small farm community. But any map of the region told Gettysburg's real importance, a point of convergence of nine major roads serving that entire region of south central Pennsylvania. Meade could see this as well, and abandoned plans to fight along the Pipe Creek line in Maryland, ordering his corps commanders to march to Gettysburg.

Sketch by Charles W. Reed.

On the early morning of July 1, 1863, Union General John Buford helped make up Meade's mind where to fight when his cavalry division ran head-on into the vanguard of Hill's corps, which was indeed seeking some new shoes. Buford organized a bitter resistance by his outnumbered troopers. The old Indian fighter's goal was to buy time for the Union infantry to come up and defend what he could see was a strong position on the hills and ridges south and east of Gettysburg.

Meade's goal was first not to lose, and second to drive Lee's army from the north. Lee had a more sophisticated strategic sense of what the coming battle represented. He knew that strictly speaking, the South couldn't defeat the North, but that a successful battle in the north might cause the Lincoln Administration to give up, might

In one of the few contemporary depictions of Pickett's famous charge, Alfred Waud sketched Union troops of Colonel Norman Hall's brigade (right) rushing to the defense of the stone wall on Cemetery Ridge. A disabled cannon from Lieutenant Alonzo Cushing's battery is visible at center. LC USZ62-7030

even cause the hesitant European powers to recognize the South's independence. These differing interpretations of their missions helped dictate the tactics of the battle to come, with Meade content to stay on the defensive, and Lee feeling compelled to bring the fight to Meade.

Thanks to the determination of Buford's men north of town, Hill's Confederates were delayed long enough for the Union's First and Eleventh Corps to reach the field. First Corps commander John Reynolds, a highly regarded professional many thought should have replaced Hooker, immediately threw his men against the rapidly arriving Confederates. But Reynolds was soon killed in a battle that also decimated the Union's famed Iron Brigade.

Federal command then devolved on the Eleventh Corps' Oliver Howard, a pious and brave young West Pointer who lost an arm on the Peninsula, but had managed to ignore hours of repeated warnings at Chancellorsville that Jackson and his men were about to crash upon his rear and flank. At Gettysburg, Howard and his hard-luck Eleventh Corps suffered a repeat of this humiliating defeat, overwhelmed by attacks from their front, flank, and rear.

As Hill's corps pushed the Union First and Eleventh from the west, Dick Ewell suddenly arrived from the north and east in a maneuver that, had it been planned, could not have been more perfectly executed. The result was another disastrous rout of major elements of the Union Army. But this time, unlike at Chancellorsville, the Union commanders kept their wits and the high ground safeguarded by Buford became a rallying point for Union troops streaming through Gettysburg.

There, on Cemetery Hill, Howard, Abner Doubleday, and other leaders struggled to reorganize the shattered Union forces. Salvation arrived in the form of the charismatic Second Corps leader Winfield Scott Hancock, sent ahead by Meade to command until the rest of the army could arrive. Hancock found the position an admirable one and sent word back to Meade: the battle should be at Gettysburg.

At this point, had the available Confederate troops pressed their advantage, historians agree that Cemetery Hill and the ridge to its south would have been swept of Union troops and Gettysburg might have been over almost before it truly began. But Lee had given strict orders not to start a big fight without the whole army being in position, and to his everlasting regret Dick Ewell refused his subordinates' pleas to keep up the attack. The Confederates waited for Lee and their comrades, and while they did, Meade and the bulk of the Union Army arrived on the field.

The morning of the second day, July 2, found the two armies almost at full strength and aligned parallel to each other along two ridges south of Gettysburg. At their midpoint, the armies were about a mile apart, Lee to the west along Seminary Ridge, while Meade and the Army of the Potomac looked down from the east, along Cemetery Ridge. But on the right of the union flank, up on what became known as "The Fishhook" of Cemetery Hill and Culp's Hill, just south of town, Ewell's men were within rifle shot and eyesight of the Union lines. This focused Meade's attention on his right, as Lee hoped, while Lee spent the morning trying to convince Longstreet that the Union line was unsupported on its left flank, and an attack from the west would win the battle.

A strange spirit of dissatisfaction had come over Longstreet, a bluff "Old Army" regular and staunch defensive fighter. With the aggressive Jackson, he had

Historian John B. Bachelder prepared this 1880 plat, one of four sequential surveys of the cavalry battle that occurred east of Gettysburg on July 3, 1863. It depicts J.E.B. Stuart's Confederate horsemen massing for an assault on General Gregg's Federal troopers.

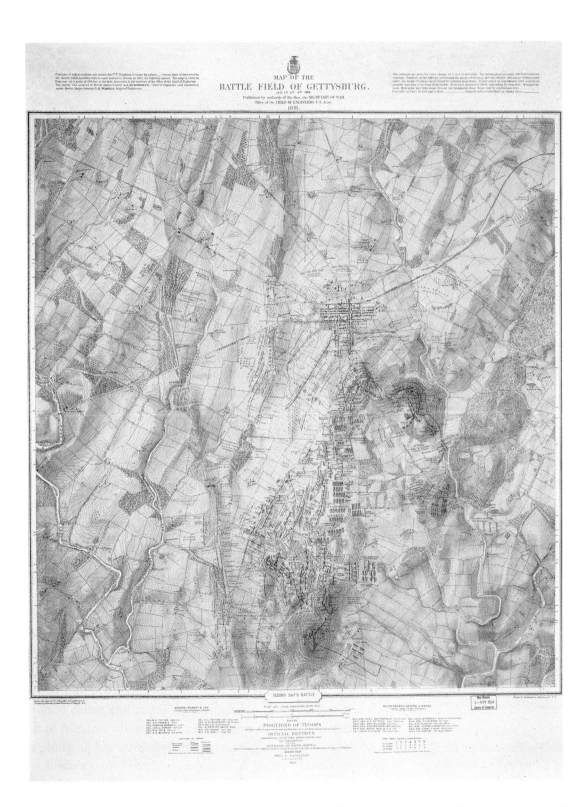

Thirteen years after Gettysburg, John Bachelder provided the research for a complex and remarkably accurate series of maps that detailed brigade and regimental positions on each of the three days of battle. The terrain features were based on a postwar survey made by General G.K. Warren, Meade's Chief Topographical Engineer during the battle.

given Lee and the Army of Northern Virginia a combination of tactical and strategic thinking that the Army of the Potomac had never been able to overcome. But Jackson was gone, and Longstreet didn't want to make this fight. "Old Pete" bitterly argued that Lee should leave Gettysburg and seek better ground, in hopes of forcing Meade to attack, in hopes of another Fredericksburg.

Finally, after hours of delay caused by poor staff work and tardy orders, Longstreet got under way, only to encounter a situation that has become one of the most remarkable controversies in American military history: the left center of the secure Union line on Cemetery Ridge was commanded by former congressman Daniel Sickles, a "War Democrat" whose support was needed by Lincoln.

Sickles's contribution to the history of Gettysburg was moving his entire corps, the Third, out of line toward a somewhat higher spot in a peach orchard bordering the Emmitsburg Road. By the time a horrified Meade could react, Longstreet's advance elements slammed into Sickles's troops and it was too late. Sickles survived both this move and loss of his leg to ever-after claim that he had personally broken up Longstreet's attack, and thus saved the Union victory.

In reality, Meade's victory that day stemmed from two failures by Lee, the first characteristic, the second most uncharacteristic. Lee's relationship with and faith in his subordinates was such that he rarely gave detailed or explicit orders, thus leaving much, sometimes too much, to his commanders' discretion. This day, Lee refused to give the stubborn Longstreet a preemptory order to get moving, and Longstreet, sulking, took most of the day to do it.

The uncharacteristic failure was not applying maximum force to a perceived Federal vulnerability; instead, Longstreet's divisions were ordered to attack "en echelon," this day sequentially from right to left,

"Absolution on Wheat Field" by Charles W. Reed.

rather than massing to punch through the Union line. Geography played a role as the extreme right of the Confederate attack had to go over Little Round Top, the extreme left of the Union line.

All that morning as the Confederate attack stalled, Little Round Top was unoccupied. At the last minute, Meade's chief engineer, Brigadier General Governor K. Warren, rushed elements of two Fifth Corps brigades up the hill. In one of the most renowned small-unit actions in military history the

left flank of Strong Vincent's brigade, Joshua Chamberlain's 20th Maine Infantry, down to 300 men, beat back three charges by Alabama regiments of John B. Hood's division, then countercharged and helped save the Union line from being "rolled up."

Longstreet pressed on at 5 p.m., sending more brigades into the center through the peach orchard and wheatfield. But counterattacks, including a suicidal charge by the First Minnesota Infantry, held the line for the Union. Finally, after waiting all day for the sounds of Longstreet's artillery, Ewell's Corps tried to take Culp's Hill, on the extreme Union right flank, behind Cemetery Ridge. Jubal Early's division actually broke through temporarily, but as in the center, and on Little Round Top, the Confederate attacks failed for lack of support. By this time, each army had

In his April 30, 1863 sketch, artist Edwin Forbes depicted soldiers of the 5th New York Zouaves, a unit in the Army of the Potomac's Fifth Corps, en route to the Kelly's Ford crossing of the Rappahannock. Hooker's bold flanking march brought his army to the left flank and rear of Lee's forces.
LC USZ62-542

suffered about 10,000 casualties and the battle had not been decided.

July 3, 1863, the third day, perhaps the most important single day in American military history, was very hot, and for none was it hotter than it was Jeb Stuart, who had straggled into Lee's Headquarters the previous night. As Meade had predicted, Lee was determined to attack the Union center and it would be Stuart's job to simultaneously hit the Federals from the rear, just as Longstreet's grand assault should pierce the Union center. This plan which might have worked a day or two earlier, became the disatrous "Pickett's Charge," named after the Virginia division leader whose troops formed almost half of the 12,500 Confederate attackers.

In an important respect, day three began as did day two for the Confederate high command; Longstreet and Lee were locked in

Passing along the north bank of the Rappahannock on the way to Kelly's Ford.
April 30th 1863

bitter argument and as before, Longstreet finally gave way. Some medical historians feel that Lee was suffering symptoms of the heart disease that was to kill him in seven years. What is certain is that his military judgment was clouded by the almost universal success he and the Army of Northern Virginia had enjoyed over the Army of the Potomac for the past two years. Where Longstreet concluded that the South's limited resources argued a conservative strategy, Lee always felt that he was in a race against time, and that audacity was the South's only real chance.

Longstreet was heartbroken; during the massive 160-gun Confederate artillery barrage that preceded the afternoon assault he could barely bring himself to speak. So Pickett actually directed the placement of the ten brigades that stepped out as if on parade at 3 p.m., for the one mile, uphill march to a little clump of trees where Winfield Hancock and the Second Corps were waiting.

Henry Hunt, the Federal artillery commander, had shrewdly ordered his cannoneers to stop firing during the Confederate barrage, both to conserve ammunition for the charge that all knew would follow, and to fool the Confederates into thinking that the Union guns had been knocked out.

Edward Porter Alexander, the brilliant young Confederate artillery commander, later concluded from studying the field, and maps only then available, that he or Lee should have recognized the vulnerability of the Union line to artillery from Ewell's area above "The Fishhook." Such plunging fire could have raked the Union line and prevented the concentrated Federal fire that broke up Longstreet's "Grand Assault." Instead, Alexander's guns fired over the heads of Hancock's Second Corps into the Union rear.

Halfway across the fields, at the Emmitsburg Road, Lee's men began to feel the sting of renewed Federal artillery; the men came on at a fast walk, one hundred yards per minute, and actually dressed ranks, performing a right oblique under fire, to the everlasting admiration of the watching Federals. While the Confederate left faltered under Union flanking fire, Pickett's Virginians held formation in the face of canister and then point-blank musketry before dissolving among the small clump of trees Lee had used as the aiming point.

Lee rode to meet the shattered gray remnants, repeating again and again "It's all my fault," while Longstreet rallied the survivors to meet an expected counterattack. It never came. The Army of Northern Virginia escaped.

Behind on the field lay 7,000 men killed on both sides and many of the 32,000 wounded, a vast "sea of misery" to the doctors and civilians who converged to succor the remnants of both armies. More than 10,000 men were prisoners or missing in action, many of those probably dead. Of the 160,000 men who had marched to Gettysburg, 51,000 had become casualties.

Lee's army escaped but it was both a tactical and a strategic victory for Meade; the North wouldn't give up, at least not that year, and gone forever was any realistic chance that the Europeans might intervene on behalf of the South. When Vicksburg, Mississippi surrendered to U.S. Grant on July Fourth, the Confederacy had indeed reached its "high water mark."

⎯⎯⎯⎯⎯⎯⎯⎯

During the Confederate invasion of Gettysburg, like the smaller attempt at Antietam the year before, Robert E. Lee's Army of Northern Virginia reported few problems with maps. Even during the Antietam

On March 12, 1863, Captain Daniel Hart of the 7th New Jersey married Ellen Lammond in an elaborate open-air service at the Third Corps winter encampment near Falmouth, Virginia. The guests included Army of the Potomac commander Joseph Hooker, who stands second from right in this Alfred Waud sketch. Two months later, Captain Hart was severely wounded in the battle of Chancellorsville. LC USZ62-14897

campaign, the Confederates had recognized Gettysburg's strategic importance as a junction where nine roads met (p. 96). During the 1863 campaign, the lead divisions of Ewell's Second Corps moved from Chambersburg to Gettysburg to York and Wrightsville all without problem. The medium-sized towns, such as York, Harrisburg, and Gettysburg meant that travel between these towns had good roads. In addition, the Confederate Army also contained many Pennsylvania soldiers who could be used as guides.

Lee's biggest problem during the campaign was not lack of information about the location of towns and roads, but rather lack of information about the location of the Union Army. Early in the campaign, Lee gave his cavalry commander, Jeb Stuart, permission to make one of his celebrated rides around the Union Army (p. 97). While Stuart was collecting glory and cattle, Lee's army was blind in relation to their enemy. The battle at Gettysburg was a small battle that grew bigger as more troops poured into the fray (pp. 100-101), but the Confederate leader was never sure how much of the Army of the Potomac he was facing.

During the battle, the most significant mapping problem happened on the second day as General Longstreet moved his corps behind Seminary Ridge in preparation for the attack on General Sickles's extended position in the Peach Orchard (p. 103). The Confederates wanted to maintain secrecy, so they had to avoid showing their troops to the Union soldiers on the other side of the Emmitsburg Road. To accomplish this, Longstreet had to march his corps by a convoluted route behind Herr Ridge and across Pitzer's Run. They finally used a small wagon road, but it was late afternoon before the corps was finally ready to attack, a delay that could have been avoided with a good map.

The attack moved from left to right as indicated on the Bachelder map (p. 102), aiming at the crucial peak of Little Round Top on the bottom center of the map. The Confederate delay in starting the attack allowed Governor K. Warren, General Meade's chief topographer, to call up reinforcements and save the hill. After the battle, Warren compiled the best map of the battlefield, which Bachelder used as the basis for his own map.

Chapter 8

Chickamauga to Missionary Ridge

William Rosecrans, the Federal army commander in Tennessee, was no George McClellan: he knew how to move quickly, and he knew how to fight. At Stones River, over New Year of 1862-63, he held off·two days of frantic assaults by Braxton Bragg's army, a drawn battle that Lincoln was happy to accept as a Union victory, given the country's need to recover from the pre-Christmas disaster at Fredericksburg.

But Rosecrans was very much like McClellan when he was determined to stay put and get ready for the next move; no requests or orders from Lincoln and Stanton could sway him. And so for the first six months of 1863, while Rosecrans was bombarded with pleas to do something, anything to keep the Confederates in the West from unifying against Grant's Vicksburg campaign, his replies to Washington had an insolence worthy of McClellan's best.

Rosecrans's strategic mission was to complete his portion of the Union's initiatives down the center of the western Confederacy: while Grant consolidated his victories at Forts Henry and Donelson with Shiloh and then moved over to the Mississippi, Rosecrans was to push through Tennessee to Chattanooga. From there he could move farther south or he could move east toward Atlanta, surely a fatal blow to the Confederacy, which would be denied the food and matériel supplied by the deep south and west.

Bragg and his Army of Tennessee guarded Chattanooga, the hub for the South's entire rail network from Texas, across the Missis-sippi, through to Atlanta, and up to Richmond. Bragg was not the

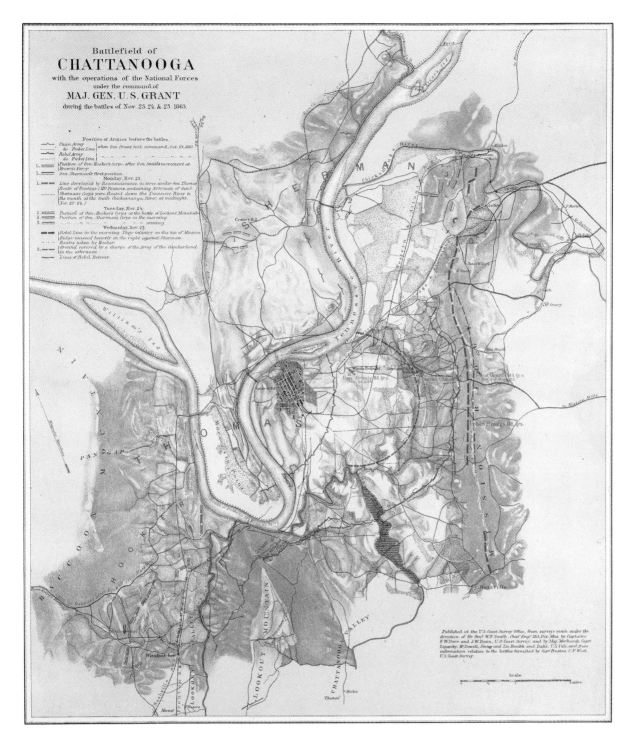

Battlefield of
CHATTANOOGA
with the operations of the National Forces
under the command of
MAJ. GEN. U. S. GRANT
during the battles of Nov. 23, 24, & 25, 1863.

Published at the U.S. Coast Survey Office, from surveys made under the direction of Br. Gen¹ W.F. Smith, Chief Eng¹ Mil. Div. Miss. by Captains F.W.Dorr and J.W.Donn, U.S. Coast Survey, and by Maj. Merhards, Capt Ligowsky, McDowell, Jenny and Lts. Boeckh and Dahl, U.S. Vols. and from information relative to the battles furnished by Capt Preston, C.F. West, U.S. Coast Survey.

Scale.

This plan accompanied General Grant's report of his victorious assault on Bragg's army at Chattanooga. Federal topographical officers gathered data for the map under the direction of General William F. "Baldy" Smith, Chief Engineer of the Military Division of the Mississippi. Smith later served in Virginia as commander of the Eighteenth Corps.

General Braxton Bragg was a hero of the Mexican War and a close friend of Confederate President Jefferson Davis but he was unable to attain victory in the war's western theater. "He loved to crush the spirit of his men," a Tennessean recalled bitterly. "Not a single soldier in the whole army ever loved or respected him."

LC USZ62-4888

most misunderstood of Civil War commanders; his men and subordinates knew him to be stubborn, imperious, and cruel.

Bragg enjoyed one unshakable ally, however, Mexican War messmate and now President Jefferson Davis, who backed him through repeated failures and strident protests by his subordinates. The troops' basic lack of faith in Bragg, as much as any brilliance by Federal generals, caused the eventual success of the campaign begun by Rosecrans in June, 1863.

Rosecrans's sudden movement, a month after Grant's final push started for Vicksburg, became the Tullahoma Campaign. In a series of rapid and skillful marches, Bragg was repeatedly fooled and flanked. Reaching Chattanooga, Bragg regrouped his 44,000 men, begged Richmond for reinforcements, and awaited Rosecrans's advancing army of 56,000. The coming battle would be called Chickamauga, an Indian word meaning "River of Blood."

Rosecrans again stalled, ignoring orders from Washington. He had help from the hapless General Ambrose Burnside, who had resigned command of the Army of the Potomac after Fredericksburg. Burnside was given 24,000 Federals in Cincinnati, with orders to drive the Rebels from Knoxville and support Rosecrans's left flank. For most of July neither Rosecrans nor Burnside did much of anything, prompting a preemptory order from Washington to move on August 4. The Union generals finally pushed off two weeks later, Burnside to no particular effect, but Rosecrans skillfully and quickly, as was his habit once under way.

Rosecrans had used the six weeks following Tullahoma to study the maps and carefully plan a surprise main attack on Chattanooga from the south, rather than directly from the north, as Bragg expected. After days of conflicting reports, General Joseph Wheeler's Rebel cavalry confirmed the success of Rosecrans's maneuvers; finally accepting that he was flanked, Bragg abandoned Chattanooga without a fight on September 7. A now-overconfident Rosecrans plunged his army after Bragg, convinced the Confederates were in flight.

As had Lee before Antietam, Rosecrans split his army into a Napoleonic "fan." There were three wings in this case, with Major General Thomas Crittenden's Twenty-first Corps to the north, pushing down from Chattanooga, Major General George Thomas's Fourteenth Corps in the center, heading for Stevens Gap, while Major General Alexander McCook's Twentieth Corps was sent fifty miles south to cut off what he assumed was Bragg's retreat into Georgia.

In fact, Bragg had no intention of abandoning Chattanooga and had skillfully tricked Rosecrans into thinking his retreat was final, planting tales with fake deserters and gullible civilians. Reinforced by two divisions from the Vicksburg area, he was expecting at any moment Longstreet's corps from the Army of Northern Virginia.

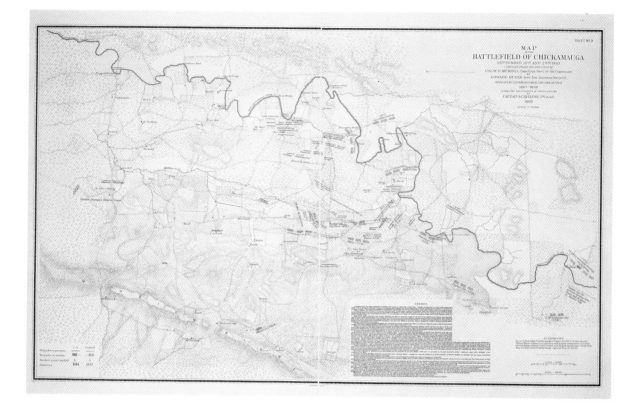

Bragg's plan was to concentrate his now-large forces at Lafayette, Georgia, and defeat Rosecrans's divided forces in detail, as they came through the mountain passes. As Thomas's lead divisions emerged, Bragg wanted to smash them into a cul-de-sac called McLemore's Cove. At this point, Bragg's dismal relations with his subordinates sabotaged the plan. Not trusting his orders, they delayed until Thomas's exposed divisions were rapidly pulled back.

Rosecrans still didn't believe he had lost the initiative and it took three more days, until September 13, before he sent frantic orders to pull in his scattered commands. Bragg sat idle for four more days, allowing Rosecrans to nearly complete his consolidation.

But on September 17, the advance units of Longstreet's 12,000 men completed their 900-mile journey from Richmond, to Atlanta, then west to Bragg. Burnside had finally taken Knoxville, forcing the circumnavigation. Bragg ordered a dawn attack for the 18th, striking Crittenden's corps on Rosecrans's northern flank. Once again, his subordinates failed him: none were ready on time. General Bushrod Johnson's men marched off the wrong way and Federal cavalry destroyed a bridge, further delaying the attack.

That night Rosecrans redeployed his forces, moving Thomas around behind Crittenden to form a center, with the whole army farther north than Bragg realized. Rosecrans was just as ignorant of

William Emery Merrill, an 1859 graduate of West Point, was brevetted major for his gallantry at the battle of Chickamauga. After the war he supervised a team of cartographers in the preparation of a ten-map series that pinpointed troop positions during the engagement.

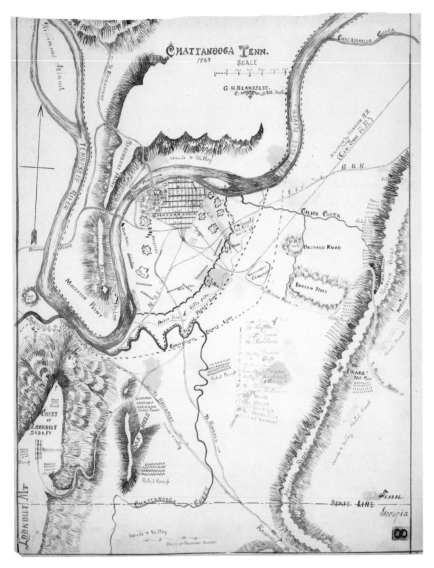

A pen-and-ink sketch map by topographer G.H. Blakeslee shows General Braxton Bragg's Confederate forces encircling U.S. Grant's earthworks at Chattanooga. Bragg considered his positions on Lookout Mountain (left) and Missionary Ridge (right) all but impregnable, but Grant would prove him wrong.

Bragg's true position; he had no idea the entire Confederate army was on his side of the Chickamauga.

The real battle began the morning of the 19th when Thomas pushed a division toward Lee & Gordon's Mill to see what was happening down by the creek. Nathan Bedford Forrest's dismounted cavalry was driven back, called for reinforcements, and the battle erupted. Each side pitched in more men and soon fighting and casualties reached Shiloh proportions. Rosecrans, accompanied by Stanton's observer, Assistant Secretary of War Charles Dana, moved headquarters up behind Thomas. But the noise and thick woods shielded them from the fight. Rosecrans's maps of the region were poor; he was blind, Dana later reported.

Bragg had not been prepared for a battle that day, and had trouble organizing a concerted attack. Instead, he sent in units piecemeal. Late in the afternoon John Bell Hood, whose Texans were the advance of Longstreet's corps, couldn't stand waiting any longer and pitched in without orders. He joined with Bushrod Johnson to smash into Federals commanded by the ironically named Jefferson C. Davis. Hood's attack pressed close to Rosecrans's headquarters when Colonel John Wilder's "Lightning Brigade" and other Federal reinforcements drove them back.

By the end of the day, Rosecrans had used nearly all his available troops. At dusk, Thomas's and others thought fighting was over until the morning, but General Patrick Cleburne's Confederates came splashing across the Chickamauga in a surprise night attack which pushed Thomas's line back nearly a mile. The battle was obviously not finished.

Both army commanders held councils of war that night: Bragg

announced a reorganization of his army, dividing it into two wings, the first under the former Episcopal bishop General Leonidas Polk, the second under Longstreet, who had finally reached the army with all of his men. Bragg's plan was the same as his earlier one, an all-out assault on the Union left to drive them into the trap of McLemore's Cove. Polk was to start first, followed by Longstreet, with the forces gradually deployed en echelon, one unit following the next.

The plan called for units under General D.H. Hill to march behind the army and come up on the right flank to lead, but Hill never got the orders. Polk thought Bragg himself would inform his subordinates. Longstreet later commented that when he reached headquarters, the lack of faith in Bragg and his plan was obvious.

Rosecrans's war council was simpler; everyone knew the army was in peril and would have to fight for its life in the morning. With Longstreet's arrival, Bragg finally outnumbered the Federals' 57,000 by about 10,000 troops. Rosecrans directed that Thomas's Army of the Cumberland, as the Fourteenth Corps was known, would hold the center. McCook would close in and hold the left, and Crittenden would be the reserve, to the north.

The next morning Hill learned he was to start the attack, but paused for breakfast, as did Polk. An apoplectic Bragg finally got them moving around 10 a.m., led by former Vice President John C. Breckinridge's "Orphan Brigade" of Kentuckians. Mary Lincoln's brother-in-law, General Ben Hardin Helm, led the brigade, and was mortally wounded within yards of Thomas's lines. The attack held on briefly, stalled and fell back. Cleburne's men then charged, with the same result. Bishop Polk fed in two more divisions, but Thomas's entrenched men hurled them all back. The morning wore on with Rosecrans sending reinforcements in response to Thomas's frequent pleas for help.

Then, for once in his life, Braxton Bragg got lucky: Rosecrans ordered the division of General Thomas Wood out of the line in the mistaken impression that a gap needed to be filled. Instead, Wood's withdrawal created a massive void into which Longstreet at that precise moment directed three divisions led by Hood and Johnson. Hood himself was shot from his horse, and would lose his right leg to the surgeon's saw. But the Union line collapsed and as troops streamed past headquarters Rosecrans shouted to an astonished Charles Dana "If you care to live any longer, get away from here!"

It had been Bragg's plan to crush the Federal left; instead, the right had been destroyed, pushing Rosecrans's men towards the Rossville Road to the north, the only open escape route. The Union army, with Rosecrans and his chief-of-staff, James A. Garfield, caught in the tide of fugitives, rushed for McFarland's Gap and eventual safety in Chattanooga. Thomas and his corps were left on the field.

At Rossville, Rosecrans and Garfield debated who should return to Thomas, still fighting on Snodgrass Hill. Garfield, a future U.S. president, effectively destroyed Rosecrans's career by convincing him that the army commander would be best equipped to reorganize the men from Chattanooga. Garfield, whose entire escort had been shot down, reached Thomas at 4 p.m. to relay Rosecrans's orders to withdraw. Thomas, who was to withstand 25 assaults, refused, saying "It would ruin the army to withdraw it now. This position must be held until night."

With his flair for the dramatic, Garfield sent a message to Chattanooga that Thomas was "standing like a rock," and Thomas, a Virginian who stayed with the Union, was known forevermore as "The Rock of Chickamauga." At nightfall, the last Union survivors crept past the encircling Confederates. Longstreet readied his men for pursuit in the morning.

But Bragg had used his luck for that day: wakened by Bishop Polk to learn the Federals had escaped, Bragg could not see he had won a great victory and refused to order a pursuit. By September 22, all of Rosecrans's survivors were safely in Chattanooga, and a now-confident Bragg, staring down on the city from Missionary Ridge, said he planned a siege to starve them out.

Chickamauga was the bloodiest two days of the war to that point: the Union had lost 16,179 in killed, wounded, or captured, and the attacking Confederates even more, 18,454. Sixteen brigade commanders on both sides were lost. And the campaign wasn't over yet.

MISSIONARY RIDGE

If the gods of war were to design a stadium in which to watch their terrible sport, they might well come up with Missionary Ridge and the city of Chattanooga, in the fall of 1863. A defeated but defiant Union army of 35,000 had displaced the inhabitants of the once-prosperous town, which lay in a curve of the Tennessee River. The heights of Lookout Mountain framed the view to the south. From the mountain to the the magnificent escarpment of Missionary Ridge, Braxton Bragg's triumphant Rebel army of 65,000 surveyed the scene.

Control of the mountains gave Bragg's army, through its artillery, dominion over the Union rail and water supply lines into Chattanooga. The result was that Bragg felt he could keep the town under siege, and defeat by starvation the army he had routed at Chickamauga. The Federals were forced to bring supplies by pack mule over sixty miles of muddy mountain trails, a journey that could last three weeks. In short order, their food and supply situation was desperate.

The authorities in Washington rushed reinforcements to Chattanooga, but neither William T. Sherman's 20,000 Vicksburg veterans, nor Joseph Hooker's 16,000 Army of the Potomac castoffs dared enter the besieged town without opening an adequate supply line. This William Rosecrans seemed incapable of doing. Weeks after the battle it was clear that Chickamauga was a trauma he couldn't overcome. Late in October, Major General U.S. Grant was ordered to take supreme command in the West and to replace Rosecrans with the man who had saved his army in battle, George Thomas.

Grant had a hard summer after Vicksburg, failing to persuade the authorities to take useful military action, and seriously injuring his leg when he reportedly got drunk at a New Orleans victory party and lost control of his horse, which rolled over on him. But the difficult ride into Chattanooga seemed to revive him, despite another riding accident. When he arrived October 23 he found Thomas already moving to break the supply deadlock, and thus the siege.

If things were starting to look up in town, matters had been on a decided downturn on the mountain. Bragg had spent the first weeks of October revenging himself on his subordinates for real and imagined failures. The generals, led by Polk and Longstreet, had counterattacked by calling for Bragg's removal from command.

A distraught President Davis had come all the way from Richmond to try to patch things up between his old friend and his disgusted officers. Not only was Davis's mission a dismal failure, but a compromise worked out to save face for Longstreet eventually sent Bragg's ablest lieutenant off on a wild goose chase towards Knoxville just as Grant took the offensive. Bragg also failed his men by allowing the perilous depletion of their equipment and supplies. Near starvation themselves, 25,000 Confederate soldiers deserted during the siege.

Sherman came up on November 13 with his men, a week after Longstreet took his two Virginia divisions off to see if they could drive Ambrose Burnside's army from Knoxville. Thus Bragg sent 10,000 infantrymen and General Joseph Wheeler's 5,000 cavalry away just as Grant felt the odds were starting to turn in the Union's favor. Grant planned to go on the offensive, using Sherman's Army of the Tennessee as his strike force.

Once Grant had broken the siege of Chattanooga, civilian construction crews of the U.S. Military Railroad went to work, repairing and maintaining the supply lines in preparation for Sherman's advance on Atlanta. LC USZ62-62364

Grant's plan was to send Sherman's corps off to the north, in plain view of Confederate outposts on the mountain so Bragg would assume it was a relief expedition to Knoxville. Howard's men were to follow behind Sherman, then swing back to fool Bragg into thinking Sherman had returned. Sherman was then to attack the flank of Missionary Ridge. Hooker was to cross the river and take Lookout Mountain, and Thomas's men were to make a demonstration toward the center of the Confederate outposts at the base of the ridge.

Bragg fell for the ruse and sent Generals Simon Buckner and Patrick Cleburne to aid Longstreet at Knoxville, but Cleburne was delayed. Thomas knew full well Grant's reservations and that Bragg's troops would be watching from the heights. He ordered a full-dress parade, all-flags-flying, all-bands-playing advance by the entire corps on November 23.

Thomas's men kept going past their objective, a small hill called Orchard's Knob, drove in Rebel pickets and pushed the Union lines a mile closer to Bragg. But the attack also warned the Confederates that Grant was up to something, and Bragg hastily recalled Cleburne and his men.

Sherman started his surprise attack on November 25, but was himself surprised and delayed by a deep valley neither he nor Grant had seen when they had scouted the area. The maps hadn't shown this detail, among many critical omissions of information that plagued both commanders.

Hooker had much better luck on Lookout Mountain. The 7,000 Rebel defenders were scattered so that the attacking Yankees, divisions from each of the three main Union armies present, advanced through rain and fog to cut off many small detachments. When the clouds blew away at dusk, the mountain was lit by campfires and musket flashes along two parallel lines.

A full eclipse of the moon was interpreted by both armies as a bad omen for the Confederates, who retreated to Missionary Ridge during the night. In a dramatic gesture, Union Kentucky troops unfurled a flag from the summit as the morning sun hit the rocks. The Federals on the plains below erupted in cheers. With characteristic exaggeration Hooker called it the "Battle Above the Clouds," and considered his failure at Chancellorsville redeemed. In any event, Grant's supply line was now safe.

STORMING AND CAPTURE OF LOOKOUT MOUNTAIN,

Major General Joseph Hooker's troops storm Confederate-held Lookout Mountain in this fanciful lithograph of the November 24, 1863 clash popularly known as "The Battle Above the Clouds." The Confederate defenders evacuated the mountain under cover of darkness.

Sherman and his 26,000 men were still staring at Tunnel Hill, over on the other side of Missionary Ridge from Hooker, and staring back were Cleburne and 10,000 determined Rebels. The Confederates were concentrated, well dug in, and Sherman directed his attacks poorly, sending units down the valley and up the hill piecemeal. An all-day fight had Cleburne at one point leading a charge on foot, waving his sword. Sherman's men suffered 2,000 casualties and accomplished nothing. Sherman ignored Grant's request for further effort.

Grant tried to stop Bragg from reinforcing Cleburne by sending Thomas in another demonstration against the base of Missionary Ridge. Bragg's luck, never good, now deserted him entirely. He had weakened his center, and an incompetent engineer had laid out faulty lines on the slopes of the ridge, so the defenders couldn't see or fire on the Yankees without exposing themselves. Bragg also ordered the skirmish line at the base of the ridge to withdraw if pressed, so when Thomas's massive lines approached the pickets seemed to be fleeing in panic, which demoralized the Confederate defenders and bolstered the attackers.

Thomas repeated his grand show against Orchard Knob, arraying the Army of the Cumberland as if on parade, and off they went, ordered by Grant to stop at the base of the ridge and throw a scare into Bragg. Artillery on both sides opened up, and when Thomas's advance units reached the foot of the ridge they felt trapped, and started to struggle up the slopes. Grant, watching from Orchard

Tennessee River steamers like the *Wauhatchie* and *Missionary*, seen here, were key factors in supplying the Federal forces at Chattanooga during Bragg's investment of the strategically vital city.
LC B8184-8125

Knob with Thomas, was furious, fearing the nightmare of a battle out of control. Thomas denied ordering a full-scale assault, and Major General Gordon Granger shouted "When those fellows get started, all hell can't stop them!"

Granger was right. Screaming "Chickamauga!" at the increasingly terrified Rebels, 20,000 enraged Union veterans charged, climbed, crawled, and scratched their way up Missionary Ridge. The defenders threw lighted artillery shells on them, then rolled the guns themselves, to no avail. The attackers, led by Major General Philip Sheridan's infantry, pierced the center of Bragg's line and the once-proud Confederate Army of Tennessee fled.

In minutes, sixty regimental flags of Thomas's army flew along the ridge as Grant and the thousands still watching below cheered and cried. Hooker's men reached Bragg's headquarters from the rear, nearly capturing Bragg and General John C. Breckenridge. Only a strong rearguard stand by Cleburne saved the bulk of the humiliated army to fight another day.

On November 30 Bragg had resigned, to be temporarily replaced by General William J. Hardee, before Davis finally settled on General Joseph E. Johnston to command the Army of Tennessee. Victory in what became known as the Battle of Chattanooga caused Lincoln to bring Grant back to Washington as General-in-Chief and focus on beating Robert E. Lee. Grant left Sherman in charge in the West and Sherman went into winter quarters with his maps and census records, studying the route to Atlanta and the sea.

———⚬〰〰〰⚬———

The geographic story of Chickamauga and Chattanooga was one of mountains. After his brilliant capture of Chattanooga from the South in September of 1863, Union General William Rosecrans turned his attention south of the city. As he stated in his official report, it was important to understand the topography of the region to understand the difficulty of troop movements:

"Between the eastern base of this range [Lookout Mountain] and the line of the Chattanooga and Atlanta or Georgia State Railroad are a series of narrow valleys separated by smaller ranges of hills or low mountains over which there are quite a number of practicable wagon roads running east toward the railroad...

The first of these ranges is Missionary Ridge, separating the waters of the Chickamauga from Chattanooga Creek."

The battle of Chickamauga itself was a bloody, tangled affair in the North Georgia woods. As indicated on the Merrill map (p. 111), the Confederate attack went from top to bottom, across Chickamauga Creek toward the crucial Kelly and Snodgras hills in the lower left quadrant. After Thomas holds at Snodgras hill late on September 20, the Union Army manages to escape to the left toward Chattanooga.

The act of measuring and compiling maps was a slow process during the Civil War (it could take weeks to draft one good map). In static situations such as the siege of Chattanooga, the Northern side usually enjoyed an advantage because they had more materials and more trained personnel. After this siege, Chief Engineer Brigadier General William F. "Baldy" Smith (later a corps commander during Grant's Petersburg Campaign) sent Captain Poe, chief engineer of the Army of the Ohio (and later chief engineer for Sherman's Atlanta Campaign), a map (the map on p. 109) stating:

"I forward with this [report] a map large enough to show the strategic movements made before the battle, and also a map giving the battle-field. These maps are mainly due to the exertions of Captain West, U.S. Coastal Survey, of my staff, and to the labors of Captains Durr and Donn... By them the distances were determined before the battle for the use of artillery, and also the heights of artillery positions occupied by us and the enemy."

Chapter 9

Grant's Spring 1864 Campaign

$\mathcal{E}$ven after Gettysburg and Chickamauga, it was possible for the soldiers of the warring sections to maintain a semblance of idealism, a sense of war as a great adventure, which brought thousands of young men into the armies. By the summer of 1864, patriotism was still critical, but idealism had gone forever. In the East, it died during forty May and June days in central Virginia when Grant met Lee.

This hellish metamorphosis was quietly inaugurated by President Lincoln on March 1, 1864, with the promotion of U.S. Grant to Lieutenant General, the rank held only by George Washington, and to Washington's position as General-In-Chief of the Armies of the United States. Grant immediately turned over the Western armies to his friend and collaborator, Sherman, and arrived without fanfare in Washington on March 8.

No one met Grant at the railroad station and he and his son were nearly rebuffed by a Willard's Hotel clerk until his signature on the register created a sensation. Wandering over to the White House that night, Grant met Lincoln for the first time. It was a very informal age, and Lincoln was shaking hands with hundreds of ordinary citizens at a regularly scheduled open reception. Grant ended up standing on a couch, in response to a shouted demand to "have a look" at him.

The next day Grant and the president got down to business. Grant was surprised and relieved to discover that the Lincoln of 1862 who tried to run the war himself was gone. Lincoln clearly was prepared to trust and back up the man who had overcome every obstacle the Western Confederates could throw at him. Henry Halleck, "Old Brains," who had alternately supported and under

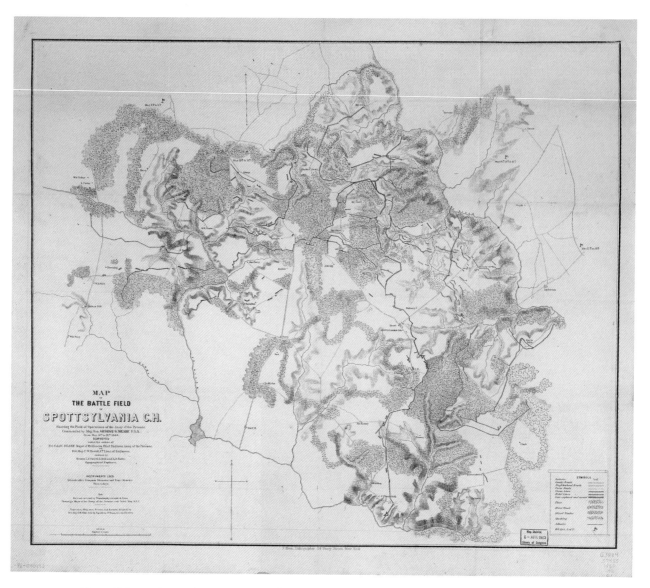

Two of General Meade's officers worked on this map: Bvt. Col. J.C. Duane and Bvt. Maj. C.W. Howell.

cut Grant in 1862, would stay on as chief of staff and manager of the logistical details.

A flying visit to confer with Sherman in Cincinnati produced agreement that the two main armies would coordinate with all other Union field commands to push the Confederates simultaneously on all fronts. Something would have to break. The two old friends poured over maps of the entire country, and decided on the strategy which won the war. As Sherman later put it, "He was to go for Lee and I was to go for Joe Johnston. That was the plan."

The Union high command recognized that with field armies of more than a half-million men, and a by then fully developed industrial war machine, a concerted Federal effort could not be resisted at all points by the Confederacy. Most of the fighting had been on Southern territory, and while the North could issue a draft call for 600,000 more men in 1864, nearly every able-bodied white male in the South was already in uniform. Southern losses were never fully replaced. While the South had performed miracles of industrial improvisation to keep its armies clothed and fed, shortages were endemic, and in 1864 the advancing Federal armies developed a strategy of systematically destroying the industrial and agricultural capacity of the South. Our century calls it Total War.

Grant decided to direct this campaign from the field, with the Army of the Potomac, which was facing Richmond, judging that the gray army guarding Richmond represented the psychological heart of the South. To defeat the Confederacy, then, really meant defeating Robert E. Lee and destroying his army. No Union commander, from McClellan to George Meade, had grasped this strategic reality. As both Lincoln and the misguided patriots of the Congressional Committee on the Conduct of the War had been urging since Antietam, the war was not about merely repelling Lee the "invader."

Grant determined to tackle Lee's 60,000 veterans with the 120,000 men of John Sedgwick's Sixth, Winfield Hancock's Second and G.K. Warren's Fifth Corps, backed up by Ambrose Burnside's wandering Ninth Corps, back from its defense of Knoxville against Longstreet.

After giving command to Sherman, the most important management decision by Grant was to consolidate the Federal cavalry and give it to a hero of Missionary Ridge, General Phil Sheridan. In 1863, General Alfred Pleasanton had achieved the first success by a unified Union cavalry, embarrassing Jeb Stuart at Brandy Station, before the Gettysburg Campaign. At Gettysburg, David Gregg and a new brigadier named George Custer had fought Stuart to a standstill. But the Federal cavalry had never quite jelled and pushed the Confederates the way Stuart's force had been punishing the Yankees since the beginning of the war. Sheridan would become the Union's critical tactical difference for the rest of the war.

Lee also spent the first part of 1864 consolidating his army, but President Davis refused to bring back Longstreet and other scattered commands until Grant made his move. Davis knew that faced by increasingly overwhelming odds, the confederacy could no longer make moves such as the invasions of Maryland and Pennsylvania nor could it expect foreign intervention. Davis hoped that Lee and Johnston could somehow hold on long enough and kill enough Yankees that Lincoln and the North would give up and let the South go. For 1864 was election year in the North, and Davis knew that he might ransom independence in blood if the people of the North became unwilling to pay Lincoln's price for restoration of the Union. It almost worked.

A sketch by Charles W. Reed.

The killing began on a beautiful spring day in Virginia, May 4, as Grant and Meade crossed the Rapidan at Germanna Ford, west of Fredericksburg, and headed into pine and cedar thickets known as the Wilderness, toward the Chancellorsville battlefield of 1863. Lee, watching from across the river, knew his best chance was to hit the Army of the Potomac as it struggled through the woods; perhaps Grant would turn out to be another Joe Hooker. Lee was outnumbered two to one, but he was fighting on home ground, and had the interior lines of communication that allowed him to shift quickly to meet Grant, attacking from the outside. Both armies were virtually blind. Even though the ground had been fought over for nearly two years, there were no reliable maps and existing roads were narrow tracks; there were no grand vistas like those at Missionary Ridge.

Grant wanted to race past Lee's flank and get through the Wilderness, to the open plains where his numbers could overwhelm the rebels. He joked with a newspaper reporter that he hoped to be in Richmond in four days "if General Lee becomes a party to the agreement; but if he objects, the trip will undoubtedly be prolonged." Lee's objections came in the form of Dick Ewell's Second Corps, which collided with Warren's veterans on May 5 to start an afternoon of confusing and costly back and forth in the dark woods. Battle lines and commanders became tangled and separated. The fighting reached levels that would have been a full battle in previous years, followed by a retreat. But the advance units of each side continued to converge, and began to see what was in the offing. The dry woods ignited, and the wounded of both sides died screaming in the flames.

Confederates also prayed that night for the arrival of Longstreet, finally recalled from Tennessee by President Davis, and reportedly within a few miles of the field. For the Union, Burnside's Knoxville veterans were approaching from the northeast.

Battle erupted before breakfast the next day as Hancock's 20,000 men formed a one mile front, three battle lines deep, and crashed into the outnumbered A.P. Hill. Hancock quickly drove the Confeder-

In September 1864 Union Army photographer Captain A.J. Russell recorded a James River pontoon bridge that had originally been set in place on June 21, three days after Grant's failed assault on Petersburg. This crossing enabled Army of the James commander General Benjamin F. Butler to extend his theater of operations northward to the Petersburg lines from his base at Bermuda Hundred. B8184-40474

ates back a mile, and as General Lee himself rode up to survey the growing emergency, it seemed that his army was about to break. But the wilderness itself had taken its toll on Hancock, and his attack lost power. Burnside, supposedly Hancock's second punch, was hopelessly delayed in the tangle. At that moment, Longstreet came into line, much as he had arrived to turn the tide at Chickamauga the previous September.

Incredibly, as at Chickamauga, Longstreet's attack was led by the Texas Brigade, surging to the front. Lee was so transported by the moment that he joined the men in their charge against Hancock. In an incident forever enshrined in the legend of the Lost Cause, the Texans shouted "Lee to the rear, General Lee go back!" It took Longstreet himself to pull Lee out of the line. Slowly, but steadily, the Confederates pushed Hancock back to his starting point. Hancock's right flank was also bending, and fifty-eight-year-old General James Wadsworth was mortally wounded trying to hold the lines. His body fell into Confederate hands, and Longstreet's aides found what they called "a good general map of Virginia" that they used the rest of the war.

At that point, Longstreet's luck ran out. Within yards of the spot where Stonewall Jacksonhad been shot by his own men at Chancellorsville the year before, Longstreet, General Micah Jenkins, and several staff members were gunned down by Virginia troops firing at fellow Confederates across the road. Jenkins, a popular young commander who showed great promise, was killed, and Longstreet was seriously wounded in the neck and shoulder. He was lost to the army, and Lee, until October, when it was too late to matter.

Lee took over Longstreet's force and directed renewed attacks on Hancock's center and flanks. But Burnside finally came up to help. A late attack by John B. Gordon's Georgians against Sedgwick seemed for a moment to panic the Federals, and Sedgwick himself was nearly captured. The ghost of Chancellorsville seemed about to seize Meade's headquarters when Grant, who had spent the day whittling sticks, erupted: "I am tired of hearing what Lee is going to do. Some of you always seem to think he is going to turn a double somersault and land on our rear and on both of our flanks at the same time. Go back to your command and try to think about what we are going to do ourselves!"

The Army of the Potomac had never had a commander offer that point of view before. Finally, as Grant calculated, night stopped both Lee's attack and the Federal panic. The armies stopped fighting, but the wilderness itself continued to wage war. Flames rekindled in woods, and the screaming began again.

The Battle of the Wilderness was over. In two days, the Union had lost 17,600 killed, wounded, or missing, slightly more than at the humiliation of Chancellorsville, on the same ground. Lee lost fewer than half that number, but, of course, his army was only half the size of Grant's, and he had no available reinforcements. The men of both armies expected Grant to retreat, as all of the Union's commanders in the East had always done after a tactical defeat by Lee. They didn't know, or couldn't recall, Grant's remark to Sherman after Shiloh's disastrous first day; "Lick 'em tomorrow." They also didn't yet know what Grant told a newspaper man to tell Lincoln, when he got back to Washington; "tell him, from me, that whatever happens, there will be no turning back."

And so it was that the Army of the Potomac gave Grant a mighty cheer the next morning, as he rode by after giving Meade his marching orders: head south, head for Spotsylvania, twelve miles closer to Richmond.

SPOTSYLVANIA COURT HOUSE

When Lee realized that Grant was sliding south around his right flank it became a race to the crossroads at Spotsylvania, a rail and road junction critical to the Confederate's supply lines. Grant's plan was simple: send off Warren's Fifth Corps to get there first, with Sedgwick, Burnside, and Hancock following.

But Lee sent Longstreet's successor, Richard Anderson, off at midnight, to be followed by Ewell and A.P. Hill. The Federal advance was inadvertently blocked by Phil Sheridan's cavalry, which had stopped at Todd's Tavern after beating Jeb Stuart's men in a sharp fight. Other cavalry units from both armies reached Spotsylvania before Warren's infantry, with gray horsemen holding on long enough for Anderson's exhausted infantrymen to win the footrace.

Both armies slowly converged on the crossroads, which the Confederates had deeply entrenched during the day, forming an inverted V pointing north at Grant, across a curving ridge. Each side sparred at long range, readying for the coming battle. One of the snipers' victims was the Union Sixth Corps' commander, John

Timothy O'Sullivan, one of the war's most experienced photographers, took this view of Union soldiers bathing in the North Anna River three weeks after the commencement of the campaign. In the background are the ruins of a railroad bridge.
LC USZ62-80401

Sedgwick, shot after jokingly reassuring his men, "Don't worry boys, they couldn't hit an elephant at this distance." Meade cried openly at the news, and Grant at first refused to believe it. Thousands of weeping soldiers filed passed an informal bier; with "Uncle John" died the last vestiges of innocence in the Army of the Potomac.

Lee's lines were almost broken on the afternoon of May 9, when Hancock exposed Anderson's left flank, across the Po River. But Grant misunderstood the situation, assuming that Lee had weakened his center to meet Hancock. He ordered Warren to push the FifthCorps head-on into Anderson. The attack failed, leaving 3,000 Federals dead and wounded. To this point in the war, commanders on both sides had usually tried to attack each other by spreading out in long lines of battle across a wide front, as in Pickett's Charge at Gettysburg or Thomas's capture of Missionary Ridge. These grand assaults often failed, and by 1864 they were recognized as suicidal by the fighting men, and the more thoughtful officers. A brilliant and ambitious young West Pointer, Colonel Emory Upton, convinced the new Sixth Corps commander, Horatio Wright, that a sledgehammer blow by a concentrated strike force along a narrow front could punch through fortifications. If rein-

**Using their muskets and an army blanket as a hastily improvised stretcher, Federal soldiers struggle to rescue wounded comrades from the flaming holocaust of the Wilderness. Despite such efforts, hundreds of dead and wounded were consumed by the fires that roared through the tangled undergrowth.
LC USZ62-7043**

Wounded escaping from the burning woods of the Wilderness —

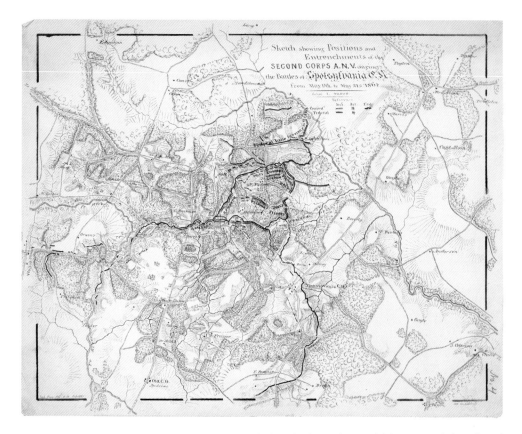

While serving as Topographical Engineer of General Ewell's Second Corps, Army of Northern Virginia, Jed Hotchkiss rendered this preliminary sketch of troop positions during the fighting at Spotsylvania Court House. The famous "mule shoe salient" projects from the Confederate line at center.

forcements were right behind, the split could be consolidated and Lee's army cut in two. Upton was given 5,000 men to test his theory against a point called the Mule Shoe, the strongest lines ever built by Lee's men.

The idea was to rush the line without stopping to fire, concentrating men and speed to overcome artillery and musketry from the defenders. The charge came just as the Rebels were cooking supper, and it smashed through perfectly. But the reinforcements Upton counted on, Gershom Mott's division of Hancock's Second Corps, had been worn out in the Wilderness and didn't press their attack. Upton was forced to withdraw, but Grant was impressed, promoted him to brigadier general, and told Meade "A brigade today, we'll try a corps tomorrow." But Lee also saw what had happened, and further strengthened the position. That night Grant sent a message to Lincoln that added to his legend: "I will fight it out on this line if it takes all summer."

Lee also made a fateful prophecy, warning his officers that the army had to keep on the offensive: "This army cannot stand a siege. We must end this business on the battlefield, not in a fortified place." Lee then pulled back his artillery from the Mule Shoe, preparing to go after Grant if the Federals retreated toward Fredericksburg. Startled Confederate defenders, who could clearly hear the massive Union preparations in their front, got the decision reversed. But the guns weren't back when Hancock's Corps started the grand assault at 4:30 a.m., the first of 60,000 men sent against Lee and the Mule Shoe that May 12.

Hancock's men, led by a young New York lawyer, Francis Barlow, repeated Upton's success and the blue masses surged through the Confederates. As in the Wilderness, Lee himself rushed into the breech, and had to be forced from leading a countercharge by John Gordon's Georgians. By then Hancock's assault was losing momentum, and when Gordon's troops slammed into the Federals Hancock was pushed back into the Mule Shoe's fieldworks. It was barely 6 a.m., and the fight was still building.

The armies killed each other all day at point-blank range, firing through gaps in the logs, reaching over and throwing muskets, bayoneting through gaps in the lines. Union Sixth Corps veterans reported firing 400 shots each in a day. The focus of the fight became known as the Bloody Angle; trees were felled by musket fire. In one part of the Angle measuring twelve by fifteen feet, 150 bodies were found after the battle. That night, bands in each army took turns playing mournful songs, then patriotic airs. In the two days of bloodshed at Spotsylvania, Grant had lost 11,000 in killed, wounded, or captured and Lee's losses were proportionally worse, with 4,000 captured, and 6,000 killed and wounded. The men and commanders were equally stunned.

On May 19, a new round of full-scale fighting erupted at Spotsylvania when Lee, assuming that Grant had pulled back Hancock and Wright after the earlier failure, launched his own attack with Ewell's Corps. But Grant had actually been reinforced with heavy artillery units comprised of 6,000 men from the forts encircling Washington. These men had hoped to spend the war clean, dry, and safe. Their illusions were rapidly shattered, but the men fought well and Ewell was driven back. The cost was again fearful for the Union. In the campaign to date, Grant had lost 36,000 killed, wounded, or missing, while 14,000 had deserted or seen their three-year enlistments expire. The once massive Federal army was down to

The Grim Reaper waits outside a tent while Union officers drink a toast "to the next one that dies." The terrible losses of Grant's campaign shocked even the toughest veterans. "For thirty days now it has been one funeral procession past me," General G.K. Warren lamented, "and it is too much!"
LC USZ61-1095

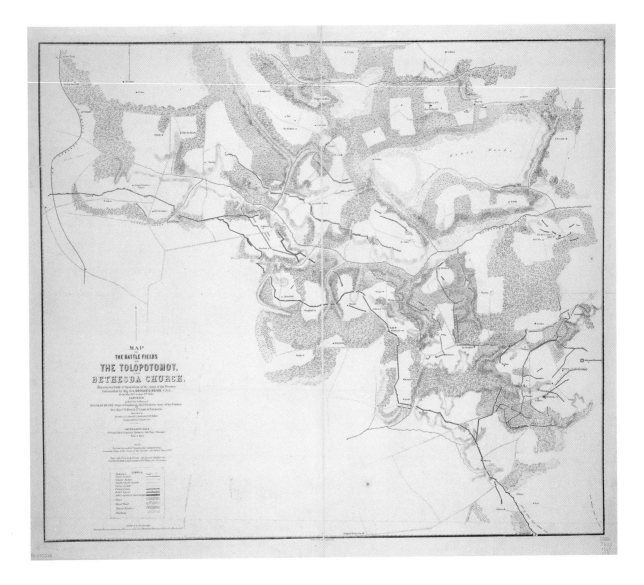

MAP
OF
THE BATTLE FIELDS
OF
THE TOLOPOTOMOY,
AND
BETHESDA CHURCH.

Following the battles at Spotsylvania, Grant continued to press southward, around Lee's right flank. Both armies extended their lines of entrenchments, graphically represented in a map by Brevet Brigadier General James C. Duane, the Army of the Potomac's Chief Engineer. On June 1 and 2, 1864, battle was again joined at Bethesda Church (lower right).

56,000 effectives and, despite Lincoln's draft, only 12,000 reinforcements came right away.

Lee had lost 17,500 since May 5, but the dismal failure of a Union attack south of Richmond by Ben Butler's Army of the James freed 6,000 of Pierre Beauregard's men for the Army of Northern Virginia. In addition to Longstreet and Ewell, gone from the army while their injuries healed, the Confederacy suffered an irreparable blow to its morale when Sheridan's troopers, while raiding close to Richmond killed Jeb Stuart at Yellow Tavern. After Stuart died of a pistol bullet to the abdomen Lee told his staff "I can scarcely think of him without weeping."

On May 21 Grant gave up on the Spotsylvania area, and rapidly moved south on Richmond around Lee's right flank, using the North Anna and Pamunky Rivers as a shield. Lee, again using the interior lines available, raced down to cut Grant off in the middle of the Gaines' Mill battlefield of 1862, and the little crossroads of Old and New Cold Harbor.

COLD HARBOR

The Battle of Cold Harbor completed the trilogy of open-field fights between Grant and Lee, and confirmed Lee's terrible prophecy that the Confederacy would fall if it lost the initiative. Grant's offensive ended with the heart of the Confederacy pinned to the ground at Petersburg, south of Richmond, where the armies stayed until Grant's final breakthrough in March, 1865.

In the fighting advance to Cold Harbor Sheridan's cavalry played a key role, driving off Rebel cavalry at Haws Shop, the largest all-cavalry fight since Brandy Station. And despite Lee's efforts, it was Sheridan's men who got to the Cold Harbor crossroads first, and then held against infantry and cavalry all day until Wright's Sixth Corps came on in relief. In the chase, Lee's men had exhausted themselves, and gone literally for days without food, due to the incompetence of Richmond commissary officials. Lee's lieutenants also were showing wear, and Lee himself was suffering terribly from dysentery and had to be carried in an ambulance. Ironically, Butler's failures south of Richmond allowed Grant to reclaim 17,000 troops of the Eighteenth Corps, while Lee gained an additional 7,000 from Beauregard's defenders.

Each side launched small-scale attacks on the other on June 1, with no breakthroughs anywhere. Some 2,200 Federals were killed or wounded, a chilling preview of what was to come. Grant prepared for a grand assault by his whole army the next day. But when Hancock's Second Corps was underemployed its men were overcome by the heat and strain of the campaign, and Lee gained a full day to entrench. The soldiers on both sides sensed that the final collision was at hand. Many spent the night writing a last letter home. In Meade's Mine Run Campaign in the Fall of 1863, veterans had pinned notes to their coats with their names, saying they were killed in action, but the fight never came. At Cold Harbor, many of the same soldiers repeated their actions, and this time they were right.

Perhaps it was the exhaustion which by now had overcome everyone on both sides, but for some reason Grant was over-confident of success, and neither he nor his staff properly scouted the Confederate lines at Cold Harbor; even more irresponsibly, Grant gave no specific instructions to his subordinates. Corps commanders were expected to pitch in at all points and overwhelm Lee by sheer brute force. At 4:30 a.m. on June 3, 50,000 Union soldiers staggered out of their trenches and rushed through the morning mists at Lee's army, in a line two miles long. To the Confederates, it was almost another Fredericksburg, and they gunned down the Yankees until their muskets were too hot to fire. Famous units and famous men were swallowed up in the smoke and flames. Regimental fights and individual acts of heroism went on all over the field which, had they occurred at Antietam, Gettysburg, Chickamauga or Shiloh, would have become legends, honored with monuments after the war, and celebrated in books by survivors and scholars forever after. But now it was just too much to record or understand. Wright's Sixth Corps, which had never held back in a fight, by the afternoon simply refused to move forward.

The Confederates that day shot down between 6,000 and 7,000 Union soldiers, no one was ever certain of the true numbers. It was a shocking defeat for Grant, but the battle had happened so quickly and with so little apparent direction that neither army fully comprehended it. Late in the afternoon, Confederate commanders were still wondering when the main Union attack would occur.

Grant himself couldn't grasp what had happened, and he and Meade ordered a second assault. Seasoned commanders at the company, regimental, brigade, division, and corps levels refused without even discussing it; the men just knew it couldn't be done, and they had had enough. They weren't running away–this wasn't Chancellorsville–but they weren't going to throw any more lives away, either.

Neither Grant nor Lee would authorize a cease-fire, and the thousands of wounded trapped in the fields between the armies slowly died from lack of water and medical attention. Not until June 7 did rescue parties go out, and by then only blackened, bloated corpses remained. The Union troops were furious, and for the first time doubted Grant's leadership.

Grant rarely apologized, and he never turned back, but after Cold Harbor he told his staff that he regretted the assault of the second day more than anything he had ever done. That said, he headed south once more, toward Petersburg.

In the month since crossing the Rapidan, the Army of the Potomac had lost 50,000 men, nearly the strength of the Army of Northern Virginia. Lee's army, which was half the size of Grant's to begin with, lost fully 30,000. Each army had lost nearly all of its experienced regimental and brigade commanders. But with his determination to go on, Grant had achieved a strategic victory; with his losses, Lee had forever lost the initiative.

In the months ahead, Lee was barely

Men of Company B, 170th New York Infantry, relax on a Virginia hillside in the weeks preceding U.S. Grant's spring offensive. Part of General Hancock's hard-fighting Second Corps, the 170th New York lost 336 soldiers killed, wounded, or missing in little over a month of combat.
LC B8184-298

able to bring his strength up to withstand the siege at Petersburg before starvation, and the campaigns of Sheridan and Sherman snapped the spirit of the Confederacy. Grant, by late fall, was back to nearly full strength as Lincoln's draft fed more men into the army than even Lee's veterans could shoot. But as the armies slipped into the bloody inertia of the Petersburg siege, Jefferson Davis came close to winning his gamble that the people of the North would quit. Lincoln and the War Department did their best to cover up the true extent of Grant's casualties, but too many letters came from surviving comrades to new widows; too many armless and legless boys came home to stare at neighbors and friends with the eyes of old men; too many families never heard anything at all. At one point, when it seemed certain that the Democrat's presidential candidate, a resurrected George B. McClellan, would win in November, Lincoln called on his cabinet to do everything possible to win the war before then, as McClellan would sue for peace. The blood would have been for nothing.

Lincoln and Grant were saved, the Union was saved, when Sheridan in the Shenandoah and Sherman in Georgia burned out the heart of the South. Lincoln and Grant got their second chance.

———✦———

By the spring of 1864, the area around the Rappahannock and Rapidan Rivers had become the War's principal no-man's-land. The area had changed hands frequently from McDowell's move south during the Peninsula Campaign to the abortive Mine Run Campaign in November of 1863. It had also seen the battles of Cedar Mountain, Fredericksburg, Chancellorsville, and Brandy Station, not to mention countless skirmishes.

This provided the Union with substantial mapping information for Grant's upcoming campaign. The Confederates still enjoyed the advantage of occupying the ground. As Grant's acting chief engineer, Major Nathaniel Michler stated:

"During the winter months previous to the opening of the spring campaign, from the 10th of December to the 1st of May, a large number of original drawings of campaign maps were prepared under my direction (twenty-nine sheets in all), comprising the country from Gettysburg south to Petersburg, and from the Chesapeake Bay as far west as Lexington.... These maps were compiled from actual surveys and reconnaissances made by the officers and assistants of the engineer department on duty with the army at various times.... When prepared the sheets were successively forwarded to the Bureau of Engineers at Washington, with the request to have them either photographed, lithographed, or engraved. By the time the army was ready to move, they were distributed for general use, each of them covering an area of 875 square miles, and subdivided into 5 miles square for the sake of easy reference."

While Michler showed how far the armies had come since the beginning of the War, he also listed some shortcomings. Like Confederate General Richard Taylor, he challenged the notion that Virginia had good maps simply because it was such an old state. But further, he stated that even the detailed maps mentioned above were insufficient for commanders' purposes: "the experience gained in the memorable campaign of the Army of the Potomac during the months of May and June of 1864 showed very conclusively that however well the only accessible maps might have served the purposes of general knowledge, still they furnish but little of that detailed information so necessary in selecting and ordering the different routes of marching columns, and were too decidedly deficient in accuracy and detail to enable a general to maneuver with certainty his troops in the face of a brave and ever-watchful enemy."

This lack of information required topographers on both sides to map the ground once the two armies had taken positions. Fortunately, skilled topographers such as Duane (USA) and Hotchkiss (CSA) could make accurate maps in a few days, time (p. 120, 126) in fairly stable lines such as Spotsylvania.

Chapter 10

Sherman to Atlanta and the Sea

William T. Sherman would have been amused but not surprised to learn that for modern Americans North and South he is the universal bogeyman of the Civil War. While he was a man of some pretensions, he had few illusions, and acted with unusual clarity of concept and purpose.

From the war's onset, Sherman's basic premise was that by secession, the Southern people, soldiers and civilians, had betrayed the meaning of American democracy. In so doing, they had violated the spiritual integrity of the Union. In this idea he and Lincoln agreed, although it was not discussed.

The war made Sherman angry, and he early determined that it would be necessary to punish the people of the South in order to persuade them to stop fighting. His passion stemmed also from a sense of rejected affections: Sherman had lived and worked in the deep South for many years before the war, and genuinely liked the people.

A social conservative, Sherman had no sympathy for notions of racial equality. He was head of what became Louisiana State University when the Union started to break up, and he was crushed by what he saw as the South's failure to correctly analyze its best interests.

Sherman claimed to hate both journalists and politicians, although he assiduously played politics through his powerful brother, Senator John Sherman of Ohio. Sherman persecuted journalists critical of him, but managed to befriend reporters and editors with whom he agreed.

Sherman's best friend during and after the war was U.S. Grant,

Colonel William E. Merrill's "Map of Northern Georgia" was printed at Army of the Cumberland headquarters and distributed to every senior officer prior to General Sherman's great offensive against Atlanta. The copy shown here was carried by Sherman himself throughout the Atlanta campaign.

and while Grant didn't share Sherman's intellectual approach to things, the two agreed totally on a clear-sighted and ruthless prosecution of the war. This was reflected in Grant's brief orders to Sherman following their March, 1864 conference to outline the Union's coordinated assault against the armies of the Confederacy. Noting that he would stay with the Army of the Potomac and focus on Robert E. Lee, Grant told Sherman, "You I propose to move against Johnston's army, to break it up, and to get into the interior of the enemy's country as far as you can, inflicting all the damage you can against their war resources." Nothing could be clearer than that, and it is exactly what Sherman spent the next year doing.

Joseph E. Johnston, beloved of his men but loathed by Jefferson Davis, was once again in charge of a principal Confederate field army. Following Braxton Bragg's humiliation at Missionary Ridge, Davis could find no other general with Johnston's rank, abilities and prestige. Johnston spent the winter months of 1863-4 reorganizing and re-equipping his demoralized army, and trying to lure back thousands of deserters with home leave and amnesty policies. It worked, and by spring Johnston's Army of Tennessee was up to 45,000 with reinforcements on the way.

Sherman early recognized that he could "go for Johnston" best by going for Atlanta, the South's principal city after Richmond and a

Their belongings piled atop a wagon, a woebegone group of Southern refugees prepare to flee the path of the advancing armies. Though Sherman actually tried to prevent wanton pillage on his "march to the sea," free-wheeling Yankee scavengers or "bummers" habitually terrorized the local population.
LC B8171-306

critical rail and supply center for the war effort. But the logistics of such a campaign were daunting; a McClellan or Rosecrans would not have been ready in months, if ever.

Sherman confiscated hundreds of privately owned steam engines and thousands of rail cars to create the largest and most successful rail supply network at that point in the war. In one month he stockpiled enough to sustain his army of 100,000 men for four months. In his Chattanooga headquarters he also carefully studied the census records of Georgia and South Carolina, and knew precisely the food production capacities of the land over which he planned to campaign.

On May 4, the day Grant crossed the Rapidan, Sherman put his columns in motion against the Confederates' winter camps at Dalton, Georgia, thirty miles to the south. The Union army consisted of George Thomas's 60,000-man Army of the Cumberland, John Schofield's 14,000-man Army of the Ohio, and James B. McPherson's 30,000-man Army of the Tennessee. Johnston knew they were coming, of course, and had posted his forces in very strong defensive positions along an 800-foot-high escarpment called Rocky Face Ridge.

The question for Sherman was how to flank it, and for Johnston on which flank to anticipate the attack. This set the pattern for the campaign all the way Atlanta: Johnston keeping on the defensive, hoping for a mistake to provide him with an opportunity to counterpunch, Sherman pushing and probing, trying to get between Johnston and the city.

Sherman sent McPherson's troops, his old command, south and behind the ridge to Resaca. This would force Johnston out and trap him between the Federal forces. McPherson was a favorite of both Sherman and Grant, and to that point in the war had shown great initiative.

The plan worked perfectly at first, as McPherson led his men swiftly through Snake Creek Gap for the race to Resaca, 15 miles south of Dalton. Five miles from the town McPherson sent back word to Sherman and it appeared that the campaign might be ended quickly: "I've got Joe Johnston dead!" Sherman exulted.

Unfortunately for Sherman reinforcements ordered to Johnston had arrived in Resaca, 4,000 men from General Leonidas Polk's army, and more help was on the way. McPherson stalled, and not knowing the real numbers against him, called off his attack and retreated. Sherman was stunned, and when McPherson rejoined the main army said, "Well, Mac, you have missed the opportunity of your life."

McPherson's failure doomed the armies to a bloody two months

Dubbed the "Stonewall Jackson of the West," Major General Patrick R. Cleburne was an Irish-born veteran of the British Army who became one of the most intrepid and dynamic leaders the Confederacy produced. He died in General Hood's senseless assault at Franklin, Tennessee on November 30, 1864. LC USZ62-12995

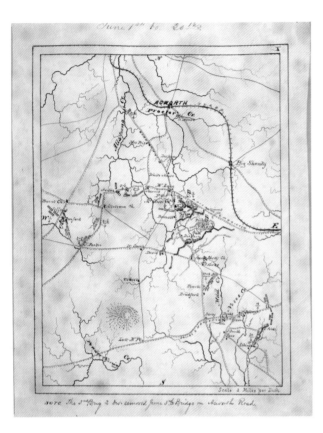

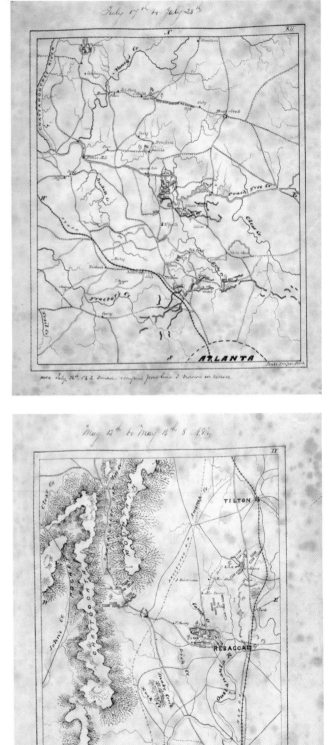

These maps are all from the manuscript atlas drawn by Major R.M. McDowell, Chief Topographical Engineer, Left Wing, Army of Georgia.

of battles along the rail lines into Atlanta. On Friday the 13th, Johnston got his entire army into the lines at Resaca; with Polk's men, he was now up to 66,000, about half Sherman's strength. For the next three days the armies fought to no particular effect, save to bolster John Bell Hood's reputation and ambitions, when his counterattack pushed the Federal lines back one mile.

At this point Johnston misunderstood the gravity of a probe south by McPherson, and started to withdraw down the railroad to Cassville. Sherman sent his three wings along behind, with Schofield swinging far to the east. Johnston thought he could pounce on Schofield and smash the small force before concentrating on the main threat at Kingston.

Hood had been conducting a secret correspondence with Davis recommending such an aggressive move, and criticizing Johnston as too defensive. But when ordered to attack Schofield, Hood and Polk persuaded Johnston to give it up, "a step which I have regretted ever since," Johnston wrote in his memoirs.

Sherman also was feeling conservative, and after inspecting Johnston's lines at Cassville, ordered another flanking movement with his three armies to converge at a small crossroads named Dallas. This set in motion a four day series of bloody and inconclusive battles around New Hope Church, Dallas and Pickett's Mill, a group of fights in the woods the soldiers came to call the Hell Hole.

Hood somewhat redeemed himself at New Hope Church, as the Confederates shot down 1,600 of Joseph Hooker's men, while losing less than half that number. Sherman suffered the same losses at Pickett's Mill when Oliver Howard mistakenly thought he had flanked the Confederate line. In fact he was striking the middle of Patrick Cleburne's force.

Johnston concluded from the first two fights that Sherman's right flank might be vulnerable and ordered William J. Hardee to attack what turned out to be the main line of John Logan's Twenty-fifth Corps, at Dallas. The momentum of surprise drove the Federals back at first, but "Black Jack" Logan, a fierce fighter and the best of the "War Democrat" generals, rushed into a confused mass of troops shouting "Damn your regiments! Damn your officers! Forward and yell like hell!" Logan was shot in the arm but stayed on his horse as his men rallied and the lines held.

The Confederates stayed on until June 1, when McPherson pulled his wing out of the lines to follow Sherman on another flanking movement to the south. Sherman was trying to regain the Western & Atlantic rail line, hoping to cut off Johnston at Marietta, just thirty miles from Atlanta. But Johnston won the race, and established a very strong defensive position at Kennesaw Mountain: there, on June 27, Sherman made his only serious tactical error of the campaign.

Kennesaw was the fourth in a series of mountains in a ten-mile Confederate position running through rough country. Johnston had impressed slaves digging trenches for weeks, and artillery was well posted. Sherman arrived in the area, which he called "the key to the whole country," after a thirty-day campaign in which Johnston had inflicted 9,200 casualties, slightly more than Sherman's men had gunned down. But where Sherman received the 9,000 soldiers of Frank Blair's Seventeenth Corps as reinforcements, far fewer troops came up to Johnston's army.

In one of the war's more macabre incidents, Sherman on June 14 spotted a group of Confederate officers on Pine Mountain, obviously watching him. He ordered a battery to

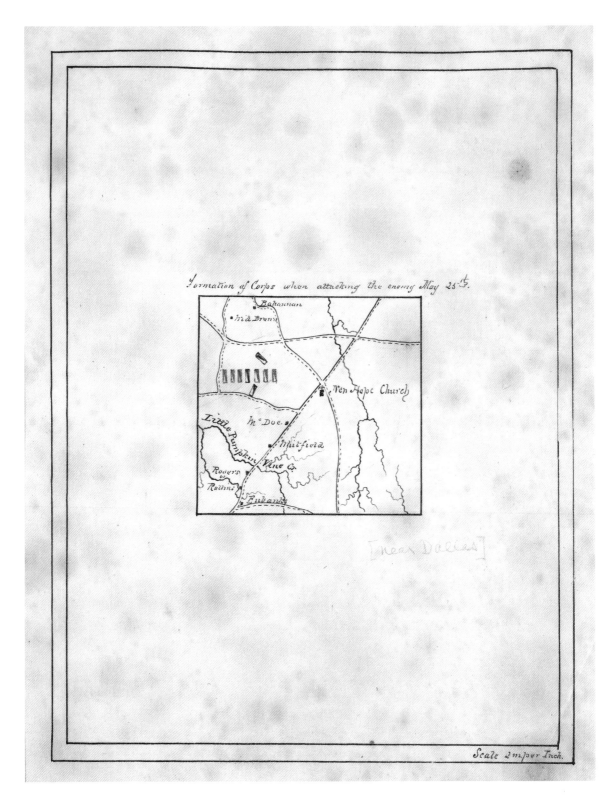

The dispositions of General Hooker's Twentieth Corps in the failed Union assault at New Hope Church are depicted on one of 58 maps assembled and bound in atlas form by Captain Robert M. McDowell, Chief Topographical Engineer of the Left Wing, Army of Georgia.

"make 'em take cover" with a few rounds. The second salvo sent a shell crashing through Leonidas Polk, who had lagged Generals Johnston and Hardee in their hasty retreat from the exposed position. Polk's death was a devastating blow to the morale of his army.

Heavy rains combined with the terrain and Johnston's defenses to slow the Federals; Sherman had to resort to trench warfare, hiring newly freed slaves for $10 a month to dig at night while the troops rested. Days of hard skirmishing saw the Rebels slowly pull back to a five-mile-long position anchored on either side of Kennesaw Mountain.

The Federal position at Kolb's Farm was very strong, with two army corps well dug in. Hood had no orders to attack, and never explained his decision to do so. Neither did he ask Johnston's permission nor scout the position before ordering his men in. The Federals knew he was coming, and outnumbered him 14,000 to 11,000. The attack was fiercely made and even more fiercely thrown back, Hood losing 1,000 men, something he concealed in his later report to Johnston.

Sherman's frustration grew over the next week as the rain-softened roads kept him from flanking to the south, while Hood blocked him to the north. He finally resolved to charge Johnston's Kennesaw bastion. This great tactical risk seemed sensible to Sherman, who mistakenly calculated that Johnston and his army were demoralized by the steady retreats and the fighting in the Hell Hole.

On June 27, the 200 guns of Sherman's artillery shattered the first sunny morning in days, and his eight-mile-wide battle line advanced. The Confederates were not deceived, and directed their counterfire against selected units coming out of the woods in front. The main Union assaults were made by Logan's Fifteenth Corps against Samuel French's position on Little Kennesaw and Pidgeon Hill, to the north, while Howard's Fourth and John Palmer's Fourteenth Corps came at Patrick Cleburne and Frank Cheatham to the right center, farther south.

Logan's attack was slowed by ditches, rocks, and spiked logs, and its momentum was lost by the time the men reached the main Confederate positions. French's artillery on Little Kennesaw blasted them as they approached and the drive stalled, accomplishing nothing at a loss of more than 500 in killed and wounded.

From his headquarters on Signal Hill Sherman could see by noon that Thomas's grand assault had failed; nearly 3,000 of his men had been shot and nothing gained. Still, he twice asked Thomas about renewing the effort, only to be told "One or two more such assaults would use up this army." Ironically, the failures masked what was supposed to be a diversion by Schofield's army around Kennesaw's southern flank.

When Schofield arrived he discovered that he had actually turned the flank, and immediately sent two brigades to establish a bridgehead across Olley's Creek. By July 2, Sherman felt the roads had dried enough for McPherson's Corps to reinforce Schofield to the south. Johnston saw the threat, and abandoned Kennesaw for new positions near Smyrna, north of the Chattahoochie River.

Another flanking move drove Johnston to even stronger lines at Vining's Station, and when Sherman arrived to scout the position on July 5 he was thrilled to see Atlanta's church spires, shimmering in the summer heat just five miles away. Sherman resolved on what turned out to be his last great flanking maneuver against Johnston, who learned of his danger on July 9, and immediately pulled out across the Chattahoochee. His back was to Atlanta.

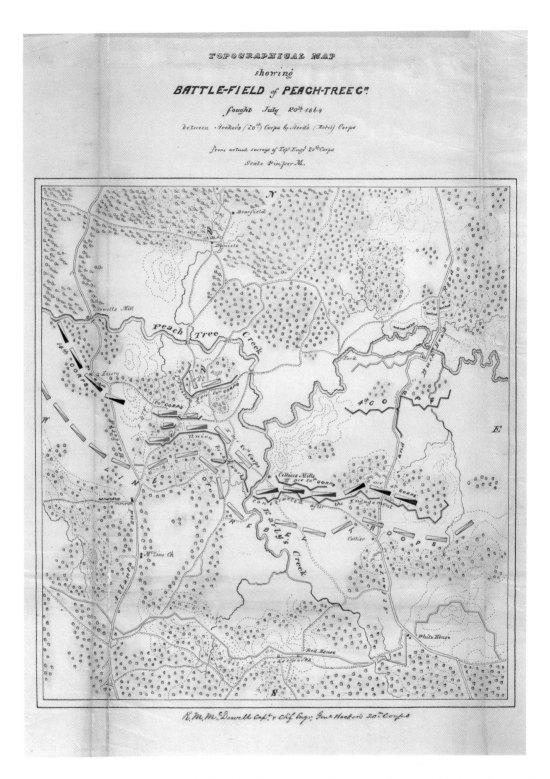

Captain McDowell's topographical map of the July 20, 1864 battle of Peachtree Creek portrays Hood's partially successful but costly counterattack on the Federal Fourteenth and Twentieth Corps. Hood would launch more assaults in the following week, but Atlanta was doomed.

Sherman wired Washington "we now commence the real game," and spent a week bringing up supplies and consolidating his position. In Atlanta panic prevailed; civilians loaded their belongings on any wagon or cart they could find, and fled. Jefferson Davis sent Braxton Bragg, now his personal military adviser, racing down to talk with Johnston. Bragg and Johnston hated each other, and the conferences were a failure.

Hood met with Bragg repeatedly, undermining any remaining confidence Davis might have had in Johnston with selective reports on the tactics used against Sherman. Johnston refused to share his plans with Davis, and on July 17, the day Sherman moved against Atlanta, he was fired. The new commander of the Army of Tennessee was John Bell Hood.

ATLANTA

Johnston's removal stunned both his army and Hood, who actually signed a petition asking that Johnston stay in command until the battle of Atlanta was fought. Hood clearly understood the army's peril, and didn't want the responsibility. One who did, corps commander William J. Hardee, was infuriated over Hood's selection and tried to resign, but Davis turned that request down, too. Davis was tired of the strategy of retreat, and agreed with the assessment of Hood given Sherman by McPherson and Schofield, Hood's classmates at West Point: "He'll hit you like hell, now, before you know it."

Robert E. Lee, informed of Davis's thinking, warned that while Hood was a brave leader, he lacked the capacity to command an army. A problem not discussed was Hood's use of the narcotic laudanum to stem the constant pain of his shattered left arm and amputated right leg.

Whatever his reservations, Hood moved quickly, devising a skillful plan to attack Thomas's vulnerable Army of the Cumberland as it divided to cross Peach Tree Creek. Hardee and

A Charles W. Reed sketch illustrates the evacuation of women and children.

Bishop Polk's successor, Alexander Stewart, were to hit Thomas with their two corps and crush his survivors in a trap formed by the creek and the Chattahoochee. But Hood sabotaged his plan by setting the attack for the afternoon, and further delays postponed it until 4 p.m., when Thomas was safely across. Even so, the advancing Federals had not given any thought to an attack at that point, and were stunned when Hardee's men crashed into their left flank.

Thomas, always dangerous on the defensive, skillfully brought up artillery and reinforcements, and the Confederates were slowly pushed back. Hood's first big gamble had failed, and 3,000 of his men had been shot down, an ominous beginning to Atlanta's defense.

The next day, July 21, Cleburne's men reinforced Joe Wheeler's cavalry on Bald Hill, the eastern approach to Atlanta, as McPherson opened up with his artillery and then charged. Cleburne later called it the toughest fight he had ever seen, and nearly 800 Federals were killed or wounded in capturing the hill.

Hood saw a chance to get around Sherman's flank with Hardee's corps, supported by Stewart and General Frank Cheatham. Hardee was to march out of Atlanta and around McPherson, while Cheatham and Stewart moved into new positions north and east of the city. Wheeler's cavalry was to go out with Hardee and swing over to Decatur to burn McPherson's wagons and supplies. McPherson's trapped men would then be attacked by Hardee from the rear, while Cheatham and Stewart piled in from the side. This engagement started what became known as the Battle of Atlanta.

Sherman was caught off guard, earlier misunderstanding Cheatham's and Stewart's redeployment as a possible evacuation of Atlanta. His attention was focused on ripping up the railroad to Decatur, and McPherson, who was worried about his exposed flank, had to argue to keep Grenville Dodge's Sixteenth Corps as a ready reserve. The Federal generals were eating lunch when Hood's second great attack began.

But the Confederates were stunned to discover Dodge's 5,000 troops in line, apparently waiting for them. Supported by rapid-fire Union artillery, Dodge's men drove off two assaults.

McPherson watched all of this from a command post behind the lines, then focused on the vulnerable left flank of the Seventeenth Corps. He decided to inspect the lines, and rode straight into Hardee's men, skirmishers from Cleburne's division. Refusing to surrender, McPherson turned and was racing to the rear when he was shot from his horse. He died twenty minutes later, the only independent Union army commander to be killed during the war.

Sherman wept openly when McPherson's body was brought in. But he moved swiftly to replace him with "Black Jack" Logan, and even managed to send reinforcements to Decatur to save McPherson's wagons from Wheeler's cavalry.

Sherman's orders to Logan were "...fight 'em, fight 'em, fight 'em like hell," and Logan did. Hardee's attack did turn the flank, as McPherson had feared, and his Texans got all the way to Bald Hill, the position they had left the night before to start their march. But Federal reinforcements gradually pushed the advance units back. At this point, Hood made a fatal mistake: instead of sending in Cheatham's troops to support Hardee at the height of the attack, he fussed more than an hour, allowing Hardee's momentum to stall.

Even so, Cheatham's men stormed into Logan's lines, which were gradually pushed

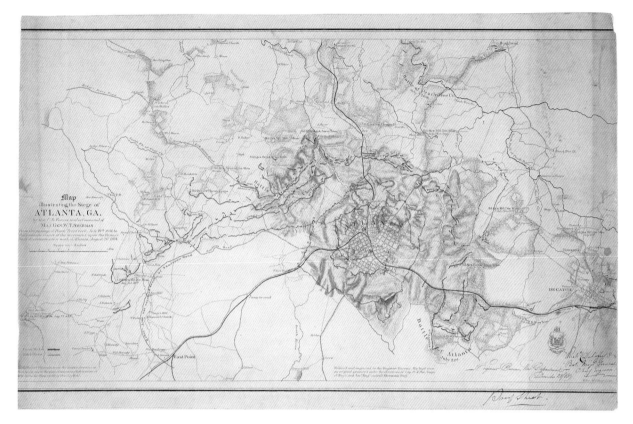

Captain Orlando M. Poe, a young West Pointer serving as senior engineer on Sherman's staff, prepared a highly detailed overview of the opposing forces at Atlanta. Poe's dedication and skill during the successful Union operations against Johnston and Hood won him promotion to the rank of Brigadier General.

back, compressed into an increasingly strong V aimed at Atlanta. The crisis came as Arthur Manigault's brigade broke through Logan's north flank, along the Georgia Railroad. Sherman, watching through field glasses, prepared to send in help and ordered Schofield's massed artillery to fire into the Confederates. Logan rode the lines shouting "McPherson and revenge!" while his troops cheered "Black Jack! Black Jack!" Cheatham's attack was smashed.

The Battle of Atlanta itself was not quite over, as the killing went on until dusk. Hood's second grand assault had failed like the first, and it cost the South a staggering 8,000 casualties, to join the 3,000 lost at Peach Tree Creek two days earlier. When Grant lost 7,000 at Cold Harbor he was reviled throughout the North as a "butcher." Hood claimed that his two battles had improved the morale and fighting spirit he felt the army had lost in Johnston's retreats.

Sherman now had a problem: his army wasn't large enough to encircle Atlanta's defenses, so a conventional siege was impossible. And the city's fortifications were too strong for a direct assault. Sherman decided to keep the tactical initiative by marching around the city to cut off rail and road supply lines. These threats would either starve Hood out or force him out to fight on open ground. The final stage of the campaign had begun.

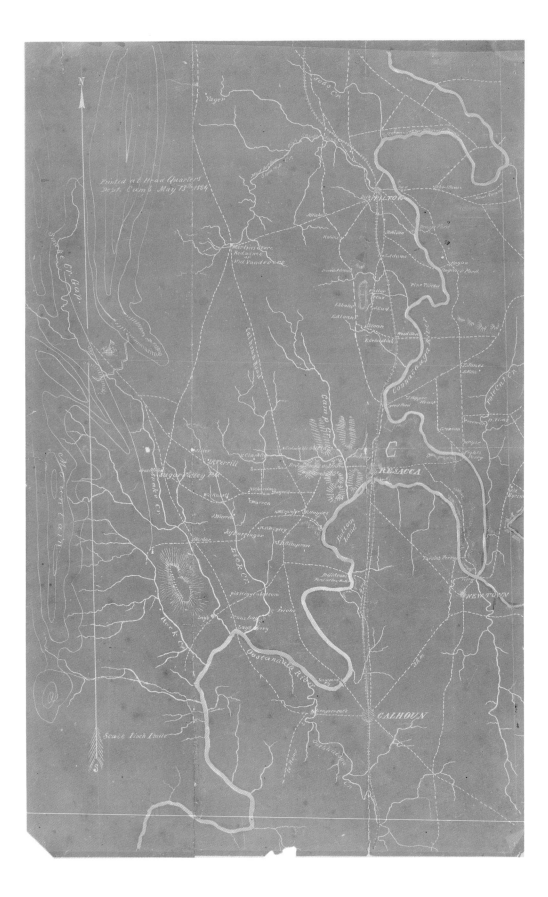

THE CAPTURE OF ATLANTA

In the final days of the Atlanta Campaign both commanders seemed to lose sight of what the other might be attempting; perhaps it was the heat and strain of the weeks of marching and fighting. Sherman seemed distracted by the practical task of destroying the remaining rail links into Atlanta, while Hood failed to grasp what Sherman was up to.

In the days after the Battle of Atlanta, so-called though it didn't produce the immediate capture of the city, Sherman reorganized his commands, promoting Oliver Howard from the Fourth Corps to replace McPherson's temporary successor, John Logan, at the Army of Tennessee. This enraged Joe Hooker, who ranked Howard, and Sherman happily accepted Hooker's resignation. John Slocum replaced Hooker at the Twentieth Corps, and soon after Jefferson C. Davis took over the Fourteenth Corps. Logan loyally went back to the Fifteenth Corps.

Sherman sent Howard out on July 27 to destroy the Macon & Western Railroad, down toward Ezra Church. If Sherman wasn't thinking about Hood's reaction Howard was, and carefully prepared for trouble. Hood had spotted Howard's movement and sent his old corps, now under Stephen D. Lee, with Alexander Stewart's corps to meet it. Lee, at thirty the South's youngest lieutenant general, was new to the army and hungry for reputation. He decided to attack without consulting Hood.

Lee and Stewart spent the day flinging their men in futile attacks against Howard's well placed lines. Finally, at 5 p.m., Lee realized the attacks weren't going to work and withdrew. The engagement had been another disaster for the South. The Battle of Ezra Church cost Hood's army 5,000 killed wounded, or captured. In fewer than two weeks, Hood had lost almost one-third of his 60,000 troops.

With the Ezra Church area blocked, Sherman turned his interest to a series of cavalry raids which were as poorly conducted, and self-destructive, as any in the history of the Union cavalry. Sherman didn't particularly trust or respect his cavalrymen, and his views seemed to be confirmed when Joe Wheeler's Confederates hit Sherman's two cavalry commanders separately, capturing more than 1,200 Federal troopers. Sherman laconically wired Washington, "On the whole, the cavalry raid is not deemed a success."

A minor attack by Schofield at Utoy Creek cost 300 Union casualties, after which Sherman decided that if he couldn't draw Hood out for a big fight, he could keep busy by having his artillery shell Atlanta. On August 9, the 10,000 civilians still in the city cowered under 5,000 Union artillery rounds.

Printed using a photographic process invented by Union Captain William C. Margedant, a map of the environs of Resaca, Georgia shows the line of earthworks erected by Johnston's Confederates that blocked Sherman's advance southward. After heavy fighting on May 15, Johnston was outflanked and forced to retreat.

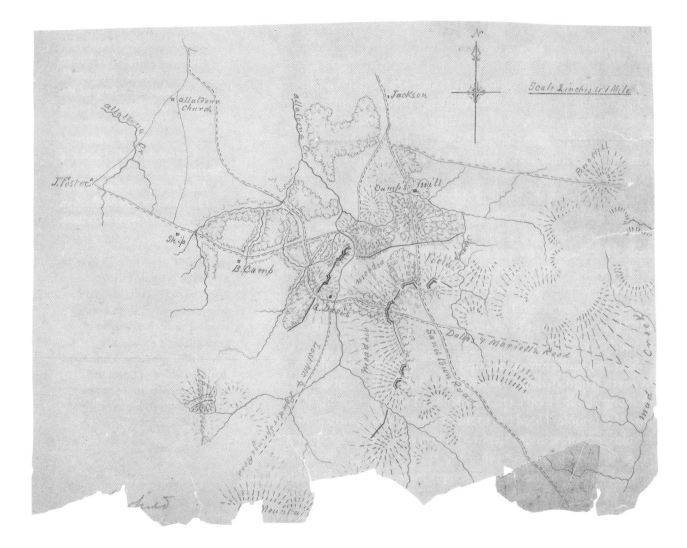

As revealed in this pencil sketch, at Pine Mountain on June 14, 1864, General George Thomas's Army of the Cumberland was briefly stymied by Southerners entrenched on the high ground. During an exchange of artillery fire, Confederate General Leonidas Polk was instantly killed by a Yankee shell fragment.

Hood tried to retaliate by sending Wheeler's cavalry to raid Sherman's rail links to Dalton and Chattanooga. But this nearly blinded him to Sherman's moves around Atlanta. Wheeler compounded the error by continuing on a Jeb Stuart-like ride into Tennessee, thus removing himself at the critical moment of the campaign.

The bombardment of Atlanta continued in the meantime. To the people and press of the North it seemed as if Sherman was stuck in the trenches, like Grant before Petersburg. At this point Lincoln became so depressed that he wrote a secret memo predicting loss of the election to George McClellan in November.

Sherman fully appreciated the politics of the situation and moved to break the stalemate: he cut loose from his supply lines and moved his army out of the Atlanta entrenchments to sever Hood's lifeline, the Macon & Western Railroad at Jonesboro.

Hood again misunderstood the situation. His army and the

citizens of Atlanta began celebrating their liberation, sure that Wheeler's raid north had forced Sherman to retreat. With only half of his cavalry available for scouting, it wasn't until August 30 that Hood realized he might be in trouble. By then Howard's army was less than two miles from Jonesboro. Still blind to Sherman's actual deployments, Hood thought only two or three Union corps threatened the railroad. He kept Stewart's Corps in Atlanta as a guard and sent Stephen Lee and Hardee to see what was happening at Jonesboro.

The battle there took two days, and sealed the fate of Atlanta. When Lee and Hardee arrived, they actually outnumbered the 17,000 Federals by 7,000, as Howard had left a third of his army across the Flint River. But poor Confederate leadership wasted the advantage, as Lee failed to be sure that Cleburne was attacking the flank before launching his frontal attack.

The first day ended with 1,700 Confederate casualties to only 179 for the Federals. Hood still didn't understand what was happening at Jonesboro, and pulled Lee's men back to Atlanta, convinced Sherman was preparing an assault. This left Hardee with 13,000 very tired soldiers to face Sherman, who was trying to concentrate on Jonesboro. Sherman's plan was to trap Hardee between Howard and Jefferson Davis's approaching Fourteenth Corps, with David Stanley's men coming up behind the Confederates.

Stanley never made it, and a frustrated Sherman sent in Davis unsupported, late in the afternoon. The Federals overwhelmed part of Hardee's lines, capturing an entire Confederate brigade. But Hardee held fast, and the battle ended at dusk with more than 1,300 Union casualties. That night, Hardee was able to slip his small army out of the trap Sherman had failed to spring and flee south to Lovejoy's Station.

Yet Sherman's tactical failure gave him strategic victory in the campaign. Even before Hardee pulled back, Hood finally grasped what Sherman had done to him, and ordered the evacuation of Atlanta. The fleeing Confederates blew up a huge ammunition train, setting fire to the city with an explosion so vast Sherman heard it at Jonesboro, twenty miles away.

In the morning, while Sherman chased after Hardee, he sent Slocum's corps into Atlanta. On September 3, he wired Lincoln, "So Atlanta is ours, and fairly won." An ecstatic Lincoln, his political prospects now on the upswing, ordered 100-gun salutes across the North.

THE GREAT MARCH

William T. Sherman is reviled by many as the great criminal of the war for doing what he knew would swiftly end it: terrorize and demoralize the civilians and politicians of the South, and deny food and supplies to Lee's army. He did this through his March to the Sea and the Carolinas Campaign.

If Sherman had died without making his great marches he would be seen as a highly successful general who conducted a series of imaginative but not unprecedented flanking maneuvers. This is what Grant did to Lee; but where Grant was unable to bring Lee out of the trenches for a final battle until the end of the war, Sherman, with the unwitting help of Hood, was utterly successful.

Sherman's greatness is based on his realization that his situation differed from Grant's, who had to shield Washington from Lee while also defeating him. After Atlanta, Sherman could concentrate on the economy of the enemy as the ultimate obstacle, not just the soldiers supported by that economy.

Before Sherman, generals thought they were doing a great thing by simply disabling railroads and purely military factories, most of which were soon back in operation. One wonders what Lee's Gettysburg invasion might have accomplished if its goal had been to burn Harrisburg, Philadelphia and all the rich farmland in between.

But Lee, for all of his audacity, tactical brilliance, and clear strategic vision also was a soldier of the old school, which protected women and children, and thought it unmanly to make war on innocent civilians. During the course of the war, Sherman and Grant recognized its political dimensions, and their growing awareness of the need for considered brutality is what made them successful where others failed.

As Sherman explained, by marching his army through the heart of Georgia he would demonstrate to the civilians and the military that the Confederacy was a hollow shell. Sherman's strategy was to rob the Confederate government of its legitimacy.

Sherman understood that an army lost mobility when tied to its base. Grant taught this lesson at Vicksburg, and both men had watched Winfield Scott win the Mexican War by marching the small American army across the country and living off the land. Now Sherman proposed to march a huge army more than 200 miles without any support. This had not been done before, and sage military minds thought Sherman had lost his entirely.

In fact, Sherman knew precisely what he was doing. He had lived and ridden over much of Georgia and South Carolina as a young man, and while preparing for the Atlanta Campaign he studied the census and agricultural records, rail, and road charts of every county and village he was likely to encounter. So Sherman knew to the ton what the country could produce, and that it could amply sustain his army.

By November 15 Lincoln was safely reelected, and the political risks of failure were reduced.

The march gradually became more severe and took on the aspects of a terror operation. Wheeler's cavalry started to hang or cut the throats of any "bummers", troops who were stealing foraging they could catch, and orders from Howard made it clear that problems of robbery and, implicitly, rape were starting to occur.

On November 22 occurred one of the war's tragedies when old men and boys of the Georgia Militia were ordered to contest Howard's passage near Griswoldsville. In ignorance of tactics or what they were up against, 3,000 civilians marched across open fields into the teeth of fire from 1,500 hardened veterans of the Fifteenth Corps. More than 500 Confederates were killed or wounded.

The only other real bloodshed in the campaign was accomplished by Kilpatrick and Wheeler, who took turns besting each other in several sharp engagements. At Waynesboro Wheeler came close to capturing Kilpatrick before infantry came to the rescue.

At Millen, the Federals came across the remains of a prison camp, and were angered by the terrible conditions; then some escapees from Andersonville came into the lines, and

their tales of horror enraged Sherman's troops. The final stages of the march became very severe, as both Sherman and his men began to think of what to do in South Carolina.

For the first half of the march, Sherman and his men saw themselves as liberators of the slaves, and thousands of newly freed men, women, and children attached themselves to the army. But by Millen there were some 25,000 blacks and Sherman saw them as a threat to the safety of the expedition. In a horrifying miscalculation, he ordered his rear guard at Ebenezer Creek to destroy a bridge before the ex-slaves could get across. The resulting panic drowned hundreds, and Wheeler's cavalry came in to shoot others in cold blood. The survivors were rounded up and marched back to slavery. They had been just 20 miles from Savannah.

Sherman's progress was slowed near the coast as the land turned from sandy soil to marsh and swamp. But his engineers perfected the miracles of bridge building and corduroy roads which characterized the coming Carolinas campaign. By December 12 the army reached Savannah, guarded by Fort McAllister, and Sherman feared he might have to put the city under siege. The fort blocked his link to the Navy, and his men were starting to get hungry as the swamps provided little food.

But Hardee's situation was weak, and he prepared to abandon the city if Fort McAllister fell, taking his men up into South Carolina. On December 13, Oliver Howard surprised Sherman by declaring that his troops could take the fort, and selected Sherman's old Vicksburg division, now under William B. Hazen, to make the assault. Just at dark Hazen's men stormed across the battlements, to heavy loss, and Sherman signaled Slocum "Take a good big drink, a long breath and then yell like the devil." He knew he had won.

On December 20, Sherman marched into Savannah, and as part of his calculated performance to gain control of the Southern mind assured the startled but relieved civilians that because they were cooperating, he would spare the city and guarantee their safety. Sherman also knew that as a practical matter he could use Savannah to get ready for the march home.

On the advice of a clever civilian cotton agent Sherman sent a message to Lincoln on December 24: "I beg to present you, as a Christmas gift, the city of Savannah."

<hr/>

In many respects, Sherman's Atlanta Campaign represented the best use of maps during the Civil War. When Sherman began his campaign, he actually had three armies: the Cumberland, the Tennessee and the Ohio. The Army of the Cumberland, the largest, also supplied the topographers for the campaign. Sherman prepared feverishly for the campaign, especially in the realm of supplies. He appropriated the railroads of Tennessee, at the expense of the subjugated civilians, to build up his supplies. He also used 1860 census data for the State of Georgia to calculate how much food his army would find on its march. The maps he left to his engineers, especially Chief Engineer of the Army, Captain Orlando M. Poe and Chief Engineer of the Army of the Cumberland, Captain William E. Merrill.

Although Sherman left the specifics to his engineers, he demanded that all of his officers work off the same map. This became the "Base Map" (p. 133) and was frequently referred to during the campaign. One example is Sherman's command on the first day of the campaign May 4, to General Butterfield, a division commander in the Twentieth Corps, to "establish your division near the line of road between Lowe's and Pleasant Grove (see official map)." As mentioned in the foreword, Sherman used specific letters on the map (the letters 'M' and 'O' in mountain) to position troops.

The crucial aim of the early part of the campaign was the movement by General McPherson's Army of the Tennessee through Snake Creek Gap to cut off the Confederate railway at Resaca (Margedant's map, p. 144). This gap was on the Union Base Map, but was left unguarded by Confederate General Joseph Johnston. Although McPherson failed in execution (to the frustration of Sherman), the maneuver still achieved significant results, and was a tribute to the accuracy of the Union mapping efforts.

The most important contribution was that all of the Union commanders were operating on the same information, but as the army moved further south (down the Base Map), the map became less accurate, so Captains Poe and Merrill organized officers to develop sketches and maps which could then be compiled into the big map:

"In the Army of the Cumberland each corps, division, and nearly every brigade was provided with an officer detailed from among the commissioned officers of the infantry regiments, whose duty it was to make such surveys and reconnaissances as might be wanted. The other two armies were not so well provided, but had sufficient organization to do all that was requisite."

The Bureau of Topography continued to be quite active in turning out new maps for the campaign:

"From the map department 4000 copies of campaign maps were issued to the proper officers to facilitate operations."

For his excellent work in the Atlanta Campaign, the March to the Sea, and Sherman's later campaign into the Carolinas, Captain Poe was eventually brevetted a brigadier general in the regular army, and he stayed on General Sherman's staff until the 1870s (comment on p. 143).

The Atlanta Campaign was one of the most successful in American military history, and is still frequently studied. Sherman's map collection and atlases such as McDowell's work (p. 136) were important to the War Department in 1864, and were especially valuable to subsequent students of military history.

Chapter 11

Sheridan in the Shenandoah

*L*incoln's preoccupation with the small Confederate armies of the Shenandoah was understandable: they had spent three years embarrassing him and frightening politicians and newspaper editors across the North. The geography of the Valley made it a constant opportunity for Confederate threats toward Washington and the major cities of the northeast, yet offered Federal armies no particular road to anywhere.

For Lee's men, the Shenandoah was both a commissary, and an invasion highway. For Lincoln, the Valley was a constant irritant, taking resources and attention from the main point. Lincoln didn't help himself by using the valley command as a dumping ground for militarily inept political generals too powerful to fire.

With Grant's promotion to supreme command in March, 1864, the fate of the Valley was about to change, although it was not apparent for the first few months. Despite the now critical need to cut off Lee's food and supplies, Lincoln gave the Valley to yet another incompetent political general, the German patriot Franz Sigel. It was an election year, and Sigel could help induce the German Democrats of the West to vote Republican.

Jefferson Davis also entrusted the Valley to a political general, the highly competent former senator and Vice President of the United States, John C. Breckenridge. The Kentuckian had done well at Shiloh and Chickamauga, had survived serving under Braxton Bragg, and was determined to replicate Stonewall Jackson's miracle by defeating the Federal commands separately, before their numbers overwhelmed his small force.

Thus began a series of fights in which Breckenridge humiliated Sigel at New Market, on May 15, the battle where 247 cadets of

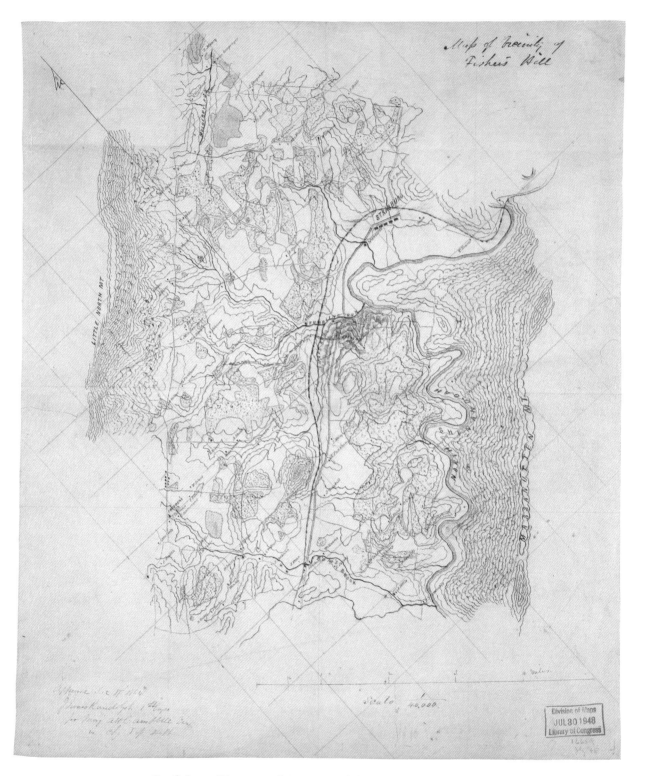

Confederate Lieutenant J. Innes Randolph drew the rugged topography of Fisher's Hill, a strong defensive position from which Early hoped to repulse Sheridan's continued pursuit up the Valley. But in fighting on September 22 a Federal column succeeded in turning the Confederate left, and Early was compelled to withdraw.

Virginia Military Institute gained immortality for the "Lost Cause" by charging a Union battery. Ten boys died and forty-seven were wounded. An embarrassed Lincoln fired Sigel, election or no election, and replaced him with a brutal veteran, General David Hunter.

Hunter was a Virginian, but from the war's start had proven himself a political "radical," repeatedly trying to free slaves before Lincoln's Emancipation Proclamation, and advocating the destruction of Virginia because of its prewar role in the execution of John Brown. Now, based near Strasburg, Hunter moved swiftly with a reinforced Army of the Shenandoah to apply his orders with a venegence.

A startled War Department in Richmond had recalled Breckenridge, and had only William "Grumble" Jones, a veteran of Jackson's army, to oppose both General George Crook's 10,000 men and Hunter's advancing army of 8,500. Jones and Hunter collided at Piedmont before Crook could unite the armies. The Confederates fought well, but Jones was killed and his force routed.

A triumphant Hunter celebrated by looting and burning much of Staunton before being joined by Crook and his Army of the Kanawha on June 8. The combined force of 18,500, with thirty artillery pieces, headed east across the Blue Ridge Mountains. Hunter's plan was to destroy Lexington, home of VMI, before moving on Lynchburg, a critical rail and supply center for the Army of Northern Virginia.

Lee sent Breckenridge flying back, followed by Jubal Early and the 8,000 survivors of Jackson's old Second Corps. They were too late to stop Hunter, who reached Lexington on June 11 and burned VMI along with many private homes before slowly moving back over the Blue Ridge towards Lynchburg. Breckenridge and his 2,000 men got there first, to anxiously await Early's arrival that night.

Hunter planned a flank attack on Lynchburg by Crook the next day, but Early took the initiative by assaulting the center. Crook's attack was strong, however, and the Federals were on the verge of victory when Hunter lost his nerve, and then the whole campaign. Assuming that Early's corps was at its pre-Wilderness strength of 20,000 Hunter fled Lynchburg, and at Staunton went over into West Virginia, thus reopening the Shenandoah for the South and losing everything he had gained.

Early and his men marched north, more enraged by the mile as they surveyed the ruin left by Hunter. At Staunton, Early made the decision that put him in the front ranks of Confederate commanders in the war: he would take his army and try to capture Washington.

Early knew he couldn't capture and hold the Federal capital; Grant would certainly deploy enough men to drive him out. But a rapid march from Maryland to Washington might let him repeat the embarrassing British success of 1812 in such mischief as burning the White House. The 30,000 Rebel prisoners at Point Lookout on the Chesapeake Bay might also be freed to rejoin the war if Early's cavalry could swing east while the Federals were diverted to guard the capital.

But the summer heat and a brilliant rearguard fight at Monocacy by General Lew Wallace's force of militia and steady veterans delayed the Confederates just long enough. When Early and his army finally saw the Capitol dome from the suburb of Silver Spring it was too late. Lincoln came under fire at Fort Stevens, watching Early's withdrawal after a skirmish with Grant's Sixth Corps.

"Jubal's Raid" was a badly needed morale boost to the South and another embarassment to the Lincoln Administration. Its strategic outcome was not what Early or Lee hoped however: it led Lincoln and Grant to conclude that the Valley question had to be settle once and for all.

SHERIDAN

Grant was now locked into the Petersburg trenches, and could afford to risk diverting first class troops and commanders. Knowing that the old pattern of split commands and small armies was the basic cause of past failures, he forced the selection of Phil Sheridan as chief of the newly created Middle Military Division, with these orders: go "south of the enemy, and follow him to the death." That Sheridan did.

Sheridan would have the numbers, as well as the organization: some 37,000 men of the Sixth Corps, portions of the Nineteenth Corps, and Crook's Kanawha army, renamed the Eighth Corps. The most important additions were two divisions from Sheridan's own cavalry corps, led by General A.T.A. Torbert.

In view of Sheridan's critical role in the defeat of Lee's army in 1865 it is hard to remember that to Washington in 1864 he was still a promising unknown. Only thirty-three, Sheridan had served as an infantry commander under Rosecrans, and Thomas at Missionary Ridge. At West Point he had been known for his bad temper, which delayed his graduation a year, and nearly cost him his commission. In the war he had shown himself utterly fearless under fire and a demanding leader.

Although Sheridan moved to retake Winchester, he spent five weeks dodging and feinting to the point where Early became overconfident, and Grant began to wonder if he had made a mistake. Part of Early's confidence came from reinforcements from Lee that gave him 24,000 troops, more than Jackson ever had in the Valley. Part of Sheridan's caution came from fears that Early actually had 40,000. And he was under orders to hold off on a big fight until Grant's pressure on Lee forced the recall of some Confederates.

So Sheridan pulled back, contenting himself with burning the summer wheat so badly needed by Lee; in so doing he sent spasms of terror across the North, which didn't know of Grant's orders and assumed that Early's army once again could threaten Washington. Grant actually came up from Richmond to dictate a plan of attack, on September 16, when Sheridan learned that Lee had finally pulled back some troops. Sheridan had ready his own plans, which Grant approved.

Early thought he could do what he wanted, and split his forces for an attack on the Martinsburg, West Virginia rail center, leaving two divisions to guard Winchester. Sheridan's plan was for his infantry to attack along the Berryville Road from the east while his two cavalry divisions came around from the west. Crook's army was to attack from the north, making the plan a military strategists' delight: a double envelopment which would split Early and capture at least half of his force.

The plan might have worked to perfection had the usually reliable Horatio Wright not let his Sixth Corps' wagons block the road, keeping the Nineteenth Corps from taking its assigned place on the right.

John Gordon and Robert Rodes immediately saw the hole in the Union line and smashed into it, although Rodes was mortally wounded by a bursting shell as he and Gordon conferred. Gordon took over the attack and hard fighting seemed about to break the Federals.

During a lull the still-confident Early thought he had won the battle when, in fact, Sheridan was preparing to smash him.

Early was pressured from the right, as General James Wilson's cavalry drove back Breckenridge's troops, killing Colonel George S. Patton the great-uncle of the famous WWII general and seriously wounding Fitzhugh Lee, nephew of Robert E. Lee.

Sheridan then sent his infantry in a giant wave that broke over Early's center and left, followed by the cavalry charge that made Winchester such a famous battle: at the critical moment, the two divisions of Generals Wesley Merritt and William Averell literally rode over Early from the north, and the race was on through the streets of Winchester and down the Valley Pike. Only nightfall, and a stubborn rearguard action by General Stephen Ramseur's division, saved Early's army.

This, the start of Sheridan's three crushing victories in the Valley, was the first unarguable Union success in Virginia all year. When Grant got the word, a staff member wrote, "He came out of his tent, threw his hat in the air, and went back in again. He knew that was the beginning of the end." Grant also knew that he wouldn't have to explain his choice of Sheridan to the Committee on the Conduct of the War. Scarcely less relieved was Lincoln, although Sherman had taken a lot of the pressure from his shoulders by capturing Atlanta.

Sheridan had shot or captured fully one quarter of Early's army, some 4,000 men, while suffering 5,000 killed and wounded. The two armies squared off again on September 22, at Fisher's Hill, a strong defensive line which both commanders felt was impregnable to a frontal assault. George Crook suggested a flank attack, his plan actually presented in a staff conference by future President Rutherford B. Hayes. The deployment took all day, and Early was preparing to retreat when Crook's men came swarming out of the forests covering North Mountain.

Joining up with the Sixth Corps, Crook and Wright for the second time in three days smashed and divided Early's army. At

Dynamic General Philip H. Sheridan stands with his senior cavalry generals shortly before his assignment to the Valley. From left the officers are Generals Henry E. Davies, David M. Gregg, Sheridan, Wesley Merritt, A.T.A. Torbert and James H. Wilson.
LC B816-8085

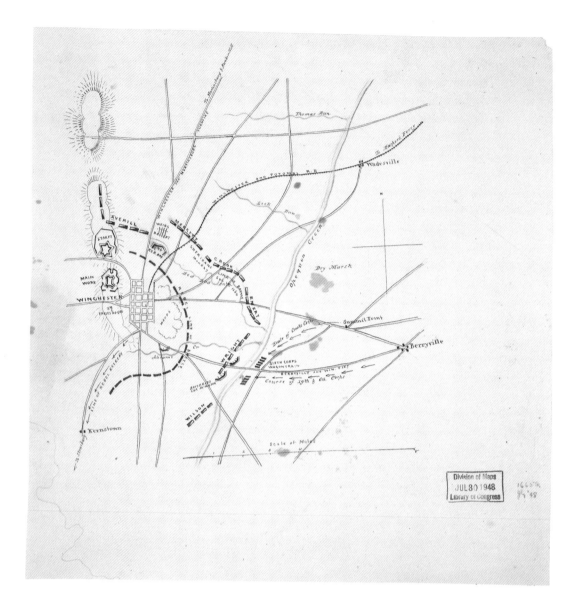

A sketch by an unknown Federal topographer shows the opposing lines during the September 19, 1864 battle of Winchester — the third engagement of the war to occur in the environs of that town. By day's end Sheridan's troops had driven Jubal Early's Confederates southward in disorder, and Winchester had changed hands for the seventy-third and final time.

Fisher's Hill the cost was another 1,200 prisoners and twenty guns, as Sheridan's cavalry chased the survivors south on the Valley Pike. That night, a rearguard artillery fight killed Alex "Sandie" Pendleton, one of the Army of Northern Virginia's most beloved officers, and chief of staff, in succession, to Stonewall Jackson, Richard Ewell, and Early.

Early should have been caught the next day between Sheridan's infantry and Torbert's cavalry, supposedly coming in from New Market Gap. But Torbert allowed himself to be bluffed by a smaller Confederate detachment, while William Averell destroyed his career by halting for the night at Fisher's Hill. The Rebels slipped further south to regroup with reinforcements from Lee, and General Thomas Rosser's cavalry brigade. Still, Sheridan had badly beaten

Early again, and a grateful Secretary of War Stanton ordered all Union field armies to fire a 100-gun salute.

At the end of September began what Valley people to this day call "The Burning," the swath cut by Sheridan's men between Staunton and Strasburg which destroyed virtually everything of possible military use, including mills, barns, food and fields. The war had long since shed most vestiges of civilized rules of conduct. In the Valley the descent into darkness saw increasingly bitter clashes by Mosby and other guerillas with regular Union cavalry and infantry outposts.

General Lee tolerated the basically piratical activities of partisans like Mosby because the hard-pressed Confederacy saw them as magical tormentors of the Federal demons. Mosby justified his campaigns in terms of the thousands of Union soldiers diverted to chase him and his 800-man battalion around Northern Virginia, known as "Mosby's Confederacy."

The glamour of Mosby's actions was lost in the Federal reprisals, which deepenned the tragedy of war.

Grant's recall of the Sixth Corps gave Early a chance to punish Sheridan, and he rapidly moved on the Federal positions by Cedar Creek, south of Middletown.

CEDAR CREEK

Early approached Cedar Creek with 21,000 men. The 31,000 Federals were wary, but unaware of his return. The Union commanders, despite Sheridan's absence in Washington, felt secure because of their numbers and the natural strength of their position. On October 17, General John Gordon, and Stonewall Jackson's mapmaker, Jed Hotchkiss, climbed Shenandoah Peak to survey the Federal lines. They saw that Union cavalry outposts were poorly placed, allowing a possible surprise attack by Early's army.

The next day, Gordon and Hotchkiss scouted a route along Massanutten Mountain that Gordon's division followed, single file, all night on the 18th. At dawn, Gordon had 7,000 men on Sheridan's exposed flank along the Shenandoah's north fork. Early aligned his men for a rush up the center to join with Gordon, if he broke through. At 5 a.m. Gordon's men roared into Crook's corps, still sleeping in their tents, and a morning-long rout of the Federals began.

General Wright was slightly wounded in the chin, but kept overall command of the army. The Sixth Corps' artillery was able to deploy on the hills facing Early's men, and for two hours, the Confederates stormed increasingly consolidated Union positions.

Rebel momentum stalled just when it seemed as if Early was about to avenge his crushing defeats at Winchester and Fisher's Hill. Many men and units stopped to plunder the deserted Federal camps for food. They had been tired and hungry going into battle, and by now were near collapse; they had kept up the fight through the sheer exhilaration of the chase.

Gordon was beside himself with anxiety to keep pushing, but Early was starting to worry. His cavalry under Rosser had again failed him, and he feared a repeat of his earlier defeats, when flank attacks by Custer and Merritt chased him from the field. So Early waited and stared at the Union lines all afternoon, to his everlasting regret.

Sheridan was breakfasting in Winchester as Gordon's men were plowing across the river

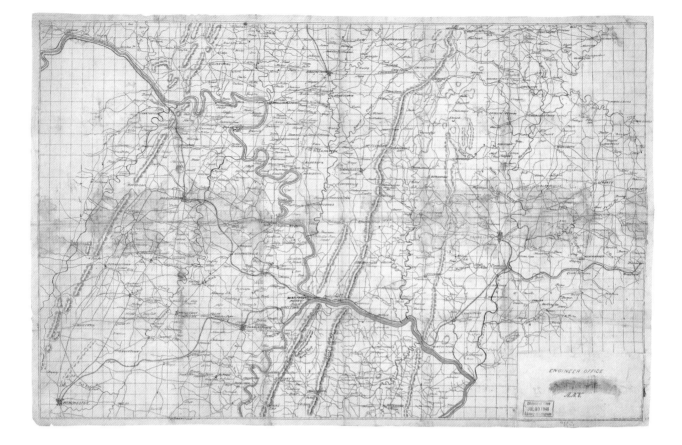

The northern portion of Virginia's Shenandoah Valley appears in the lower portion of a survey by Confederate engineer Charles G. Nauck. From the town of Harpers Ferry, situated at the confluence of the Shenandoah and Potomac rivers, General Philip Sheridan's army launched a decisive two-month campaign aimed at securing the vital valley for the Union.

and through the fog. The roar of cannon finally convinced him something serious was happening, and he mounted his black horse Reinzi to begin the most famous 15 mile ride of the Civil War.

Sheridan began to sweep up stragglers and then whole units fleeing the battle, turn them around, and bring them along in his wake. The Civil War was the last of the true "follow me, men" conflicts where generals lead the charges. But Sheridan as an army commander was an anachronism even for the time. He thought nothing of riding across the front under fire as an example to the troops. His legend grew to the point where his presence on the field calmed frightened soldiers and inspired steady ones.

Sheridan reached Wright's headquarters at 10:30 in the morning, the height of Early's attack, and found that Wright had done good work in stabilizing the disorganized corps, although the issue was still in doubt. By the time Early came up to Gordon for the fatal noontime conference, Sheridan had reorganized his army into a solid line across the heights, with Merritt's cavalry on the left, and Custer's troopers brought around to the right.

Sheridan then rode the lines, showing himself to all the men, and shouting encouragement for the coming grand assault; it was reciprocated. At 4 p.m., Sheridan charged.

When Custer drove off Rosser's troopers on the right he uncovered the flanks of the attacking Federal infantry, but Sheridan appeared, rallied a counterattack and the rout was on. "This is all right!" Sheridan bellowed, and roared off. For the first time in the war, Gordon's Confederates panicked, and their dismay spread across Early's battle lines; only Ramseur's division in the center. When the young general, a favorite in the army, was mortally wounded, Early's army fell apart.

As at Winchester, Union cavalry closed in from both flanks, and blue infantry stormed up the middle as the mortified Confederates fled back past Fisher's Hill.

Early's small army had lost 3,000 men, including 1,000 prisoners; Sheridan's army had suffered 5,600 casualties, but there was no mistaking this crushing tactical and strategic victory for the Union. Coming on the heels of Sherman's success, it virtually assured Lincoln's reelection the following month.

Sheridan went into winter camp near Kernstown, and almost as an afterthought, on his way to join Grant's final attack on Lee, swept up 1,600 of Early's survivors at Waynesboro on March 2, 1865.

Few places in the war had seen as much combat as the Shenandoah Valley. The third battle of Winchester on September 19, 1864, represented the seventy-third and final time this town changed hands during the war (pp. 153-154, map on p.156). The first two battles had been Union defeats (Banks in May, 1862 and Milroy in June, 1863), while this one, like most battles at this period in the war, was a Union victory.

The Confederates, after almost three years of Jedediah Hotchkiss's services, knew the Valley quite well. The Union troops, although increasingly familiar with the terrain, still prized captured Confederate maps, even large-scale maps such as Nauck's (p. 158). Their technological edge also meant that by 1864, they could quickly photograph and distribute copies of captured maps.

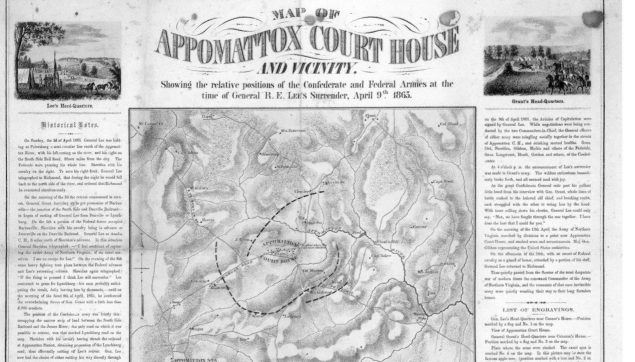

Soon after the war a Baltimore firm printed this annotated lithograph of the vicinity of Appomattox Court House, showing the final disposition of Union and Confederate forces. The marginalia include Robert E. Lee's moving farewell address to his famed Army of Northern Virginia.

Chapter 12

Petersburg to Appomattox

$\mathcal{I}$n the initial weeks of what became the Siege of Petersburg, the Lincoln administration seemed as worried as did the Confederacy. None of Grant's planned coordinated assaults of the spring were working out: Sigel and Hunter had failed in the Shenandoah Valley, and while Sherman was making obvious progress against Atlanta, no outcome was certain.

Lincoln's political crisis deepened as the "butcher's bill" from Grant's campaign came due and enlistments ran out. Substandard draftees and "bounty hunters" barely replaced the numbers, and the people, politicians, and editorial writers across the North seemed close to despair.

After the terror of Cold Harbor the two armies sat on the sweltering field for a week, trying to regain their wits and their wind. At this point Grant took his biggest gamble of the war by abandoning his front and shifting once again around Lee's right flank. The gamble was of strategic proportions: if Lee divined what Grant was up to, he could crush the Union army as it was divided crossing the James River and split by the same Chickahominy swamps that had helped defeat McClellan two years earlier.

Lee was utterly deceived by the rapid movement and took several days to heed increasingly frantic calls for help from General Pierre Beauregard, now in charge of the defense of Petersburg and Richmond via the Peninsula. Lee could see Union forces in his front, and didn't dare race south, if that was where Grant was. If Beauregard was wrong the road to Richmond would be opened by Lee's movement. He had to be sure, and while he waited, Grant's men came within hours of sweeping into Petersburg, and then on to Richmond itself.

PLAN
OF
Enemy's Battery No.5
IN
Front of Petersburg
Before the Advance of U.S. Forces
June 1864

HEAD QUARTERS ARMY OF THE POTOMAC
ENGINEER DEPARTMENT
October 1864

OFFICIAL

SCALE { Plan   40 Feet — 1 Inch
        Section 10   do. — 1 do.

Surveyed & Drawn by G. Thompson U.S. Eng.

Gilbert Thompson of the U.S. Corps of Engineers surveyed and drew this geometrically precise rendering of a Confederate battery in the defenses of Petersburg. Fighting from the cover of works like these, the Southern defenders inflicted grievous losses on Grant's army, and forced the Federal commander into a lengthy but ultimately successful siege.

Not until June 16, when a huge pontoon bridge across the James put the Union army safely across, was Lee's cavalryman son Rooney able to confirm that Beauregard was right. Belatedly, Lee abandoned his lines north of Richmond and sent his barefoot and hungry men racing to Petersburg in hopes of blocking Grant again. Grant had been at Butler's headquarters since June 14, trying with Meade to seize Petersburg before Lee came up. The next day General Ben Butler's forces tried again, augmented by "Baldy" Smith's Twenty-eighth Corps, and as on June 9 the professionals failed.

Grant and Meade ordered another push for June 16 but at this point the thousands of deaths and the exhaustion of the campaign seemed to overwhelm officers and men from the army commanders on down.

Assaults by Hancock's Second Corps were bravely made but not sustained. Finally Hancock himself was carried from the field: his

Gettysburg wounds, which had never healed, had broken open. Edward Potter's Ninth Corps troops did better, gaining some entrenchments and capturing 600 Rebels before stalling. Late in the afternoon Meade ordered a grand assault, but the Army of the Potomac had nothing left at this point.

Lee and the rest of the army came into the lines on June 18, and by June 20 Grant knew that if his great gamble hadn't succeeded, it hadn't failed, either. But instead of a conclusive battle the two armies seemed destined for a siege, something Lee wanted to avoid. Lee had warned Jubal Early "We must destroy this army of Grant's before he gets to the James River. If he gets there it will become a siege, and then it will be a mere question of time." In fact, it was ten months.

The growing stalemate didn't stop Grant from pushing with Sheridan's and Wilson's cavalry, or sending out infantry probes to see if Lee could be flanked out of his defenses. The days between the end of June and September were filled with raids and large-unit battles, many of which would have been major historical events in years prior. But the sheer volume of suffering and loss by both armies in 1864 buried most of the fights along with the dead—Weldon Railroad, Globe Tavern, Reams's Station, the Trevillian Raid, Strawberry Plains, Darbytown Road, Chaffins' Farm—the list goes on with little accomplished save the spread of private grief.

At one point, Grant had to send the Sixth Corps off to Washington to repel Jubal Early's dramatic raid. Late in the summer Lincoln's continuing troubles in the Shenandoah forced Grant to detail Sheridan's troops with two infantry corps to burn out the Valley and sweep Early's men away. Sheridan didn't rejoin the Army of the Potomac until the spring campaign, but when he came it was with a practiced group of infantry and cavalry that returned the tactical initiative to Grant.

Stuck in the trenches, some Federals of Burnside's Ninth Corps, coal miners before the war, persuaded the Union high command that they could dig a tunnel under Rebel lines and blow a gap wide enough for the army to break through. Colonel Henry Pleasants and his 48th Pennsylvania started digging their mine on June 25 and thirty-three days later watched 320 kegs of black powder blow much of the 19th and 22nd South Carolina Infantry into the air. But the blast of 8,000 pounds of powder, so stunned the Federals who were watching 500 feet away, that the carefully prepared assault collapsed into a bloody rout.

Black troops of the Ninth Corps had been training for weeks to lead the charge, but the night before Meade feared that if it failed, he would be accused by the radical Republicans on the Committee on the Conduct of the War of sacrificing the black soldiers.

Unprepared and poorly led white units instead straggled into the gaping hole and what became known as the Battle of the Crater. Burnside sulked and didn't offer any guidance, while the two generals who were to lead the assault, James Ledlie and Edward Ferrero, got drunk and hid in a bombshelter between the lines.

The black soldiers were thrown into The Crater just in time to get slaughtered with their white comrades when William Mahone's Confederate infantry and artillery literally blew the Yankees out of the lines. Of the 20,000 men who made the assault, nearly 3,800 were shot down or captured. Properly led and supported it should have worked. Grant was disgusted, and wrote the War Department "Such opportunity for carrying

A Yankee infantryman and a small child pose incongruously amidst the shattered ruins of a Southern city, probably Richmond.
LC B8171-858

fortifications I have never seen, and do not expect again to have."

The disaster at the Crater was symptomatic of a general collapse of morale in the officer corps of the Army of the Potomac following the strain of Grant's campaign. The failures at the start of Petersburg and the poorly managed stabs at battles throughout the siege killed thousands of private soldiers while the officers bickered and filed charges against each other.

In September, Jeb Stuart's successor Wade Hampton led Lee's cavalry on a Stuart-like enterprise, sweeping behind Grant's lines to rustle 2,500 head of cattle in what became known as the Beefsteak

Raid. The loss was an irritant to Grant, but a godsend to Lee's protein-deprived troops who had been fighting on cornmeal and rancid bacon.

Toward the end of the month things improved for the Federals, as news reached them of Sherman's and Sheridan's victories, and Grant finally got his supply system working. Fresh fruit and vegetables now regularly reached the front lines. In support of Sheridan Grant ordered surprise attacks against Forts Harrison and Gilmer by Ben Butler's Army of the James to prevent Lee sending reinforcements to the Valley.

E.O.C. Ord's Seventeenth Corps and D.B. Birney's Tenth Corps, with all of the black soldiers in the army, crossed the James on pontoons and in bitter fighting swept the Confederates from Fort Harrison. Grant happened by on an inspection tour and while sitting on the ground was nearly killed by a bursting artillery shell. His staff scattered in all directions, but reported that Grant never even looked up as he finished writing a dispatch.

It seemed as if Butler would finally achieve the breakthrough Grant had hoped would lead to Richmond. But other Union forces failed to coordinate and the Fort Harrison success was wasted, as was the valor of thirteen black soldiers who won the Medal of Honor for the failed fight at New Market Heights.

Sporadic fighting went on through November, when with Lincoln's reelection the Union won a strategic victory as great as any on the battlefield. It is a measure of the basic morale of the Army of the Potomac that its soldiers voted in the majority for the president despite inaccurate claims that McClellan's platform promised to stop the war. Lincoln's victory gave Grant the excuse he needed to allow Sherman's March to the Sea.

Late fall in Virginia brought freezing rain, and an end to active campaigning. The two armies settled down in the mud and waited for a spring that both knew would bring an end to the struggle.

**Though Federal authorities were slow to recognize the value of black military participation, by war's end some 180,000 African Americans had borne arms in the Union cause. More "United States Colored Troops" served in the Petersburg campaign than in any other theater. Thirteen received the Medal of Honor for gallantry in the September 29 battle of New Market Heights.
LC B811-2553**

APPOMATTOX CAMPAIGN

It was a measure of the South's deteriorating position in the winter of 1865 that Robert E. Lee allowed himself to think he might escape Grant's death grip and unite with Joe Johnston and defeat Sherman, who was busy tearing through the Carolinas. The combined Rebel armies could then turn on Grant, and the War for Southern Independence would be won. This places in perspective the tragic delusions that moved John Bell Hood to sacrifice his army on the hills at Nashville, before Christmas.

The Confederate Congress was so desperate it authorized arming the slaves, and a few units of black soldiers startled white Richmonders by drilling under arms.

The South reached this breaking point as the Army of Northern Virginia began to wither away during the terrible winter of 1864-65. Soldiers from Georgia and the Carolinas got mail from home describing Sherman's terror tactics, and thousands deserted to try and save their families, precisely as Sherman intended. Because of Sherman and Sheridan, the men who stayed in the lines froze and starved.

In February, long after it might have saved the military situation, President Jefferson Davis reluctantly replaced his burned out Secretary of War and his incompetent commissary general, bringing in John C. Breckenridge as Secretary. When it no longer mattered, Lee himself was made General-in-Chief. Still, Breckenridge and the new officials brought some relief to the starving army, rounding up meat, bread, and a change of uniforms. It was within this context that Lee allowed himself to hope.

The reality was that Grant's army had received thousands of replacements for the casualties of 1864, and all were well fed, fully armed and properly equipped. But the old regiments were veterans in name only, as a near majority of the rank and file were new men, while many of the officers had been promoted from the ranks of the survivors. While much of the Union army was green, Lee's troops were utterly spent until Breckenridge's reforms brought some relief.

Lee's hopes were born of despair. How could he admit that all the suffering and sacrifice had been for nothing? The men also allowed themselves a brief glimmer of optimism, as Lee and John B. Gordon planned what became the last attack by the Army of Northern Virginia, a desperate gambit against Fort Stedman in the center of the Union lines on March 25.

The hope was that if Gordon could split the Union defenses, Grant would feel compelled to shorten the lines, and Lee could send off reinforcements to Johnston. Gordon's attack did break into Fort Stedman. But many famished Rebels stopped to eat captured rations, and others were too weak to endure the strain of a sustained assault after months of privation in the trenches. Within hours a single Union division smashed the confederate attack, and thirty minutes later Lee called it off.

Nearly 2,000 Confederates were captured, and another 1,500 killed or wounded. Lincoln was visiting the front that day, and a scheduled parade wasn't even interrupted by the South's last assault. Meade ordered a Union counterattack in the afternoon which shot or captured another 1,500 Rebels, and Lee knew the dream was over.

To emphasize the reality, Sherman came up the next day to confer

When Yankee troopers searched the body of Confederate General John R. Chambliss after his death leading a cavalry charge at Deep Bottom on August 16, they discovered a detailed map of the Petersburg defenses. A new camera-less photographic process, by which a tracing of the map was superimposed on sensitized paper, allowed the crucial information to be quickly disseminated among the Union commanders. LC USZ62-15065

with Grant and Lincoln on the final stage of the war, possible peace terms, and future reconstruction. Lincoln wanted ruthless prosecution of the coming victory, but then a benevolent peace. "Let them once surrender and reach their homes, they won't take up arms again. Let them go, officers and all. I want submission and no more bloodshed," Lincoln said. Sherman went back to the Carolinas and a final push against Johnston, whose army was scarcely in better shape than Lee's.

The day after Gordon's attack Lee warned Davis that it was nearly over, and that the only chance was for the Army of Northern Virginia to abandon Petersburg and Richmond, fleeing south in search of Johnston. Lee still had some 50,000 soldiers; perhaps the war could be continued. Johnston had already informed Davis that he couldn't break away from Sherman, so the fate of the Confederacy now rested entirely on Lee.

Grant understood Lee's options, and his strategy throughout the Petersburg siege had been to try and overlap Lee's right by extending the Federal left toward the Boydton, White Oak and Vaughn roads, Dinwiddie Court House, and a road junction called Five Forks. When Sheridan arrived from winter camp in the Valley, Grant put him in command of a unified cavalry force of 11,000 with orders to get around Lee's flank and force the Confederates to leave the relative safety of their entrenchments.

Sheridan's cavalry was an independent army, functioning as an integrated battle group with the infantry. The horsemen got behind the enemy and held for the infantry to come up and finish the job.

On March 29 Grant sent Sheridan to destroy the Southside and Danville Railroads around Burkeville, which would cut both Lee's supply and his line of retreat. Lee knew what that meant, and made a fateful decision: George Pickett's 14,000 infantry went out to Five Forks, supported on the flank by 5,500 cavalry under Lee's nephew, Fitzhugh. The whole Confederate force would be in the open, cut off from the rest of the army. Lee had to accept the risk for any chance of escape.

A sharp fight at the Vaughn Road caused Grant to change orders to Sheridan: forget the railroad and close in to cooperate with the infantry and crush Pickett. Torrential rains threatened to delay the movement when an excited Sheridan pounded into headquarters shouting "I tell you, I'm ready to go out tomorrow and start smashing things!" Grant agreed.

Sheridan recognized he would need infantry support, and pleaded for his old ally, the Sixth Corps. But the Fifth Corps under G.K. Warren, a hero of Gettysburg, was closer and was therefore ordered to participate, even though neither Grant nor Sheridan trusted Warren's capacities. More than any other senior Union commander, Warren had early shown the strain of the Wilderness and Spotsylvania campaigns, and his quarrelsome nature further weakened his superior's confidence.

Sheridan's advance received a rude greeting at Dinwiddie as Pickett's infantry showed some of its old fighting form. The unsupported Union cavalry, fighting dismounted with carbines, was thrown back. That night, Grant, Meade and Sheridan sent confusing and contradictory orders to Warren on how to support Sheridan. Headquarters feared Sheridan was in danger, but he recognized that Pickett's isolation was the opportunity Grant had long been seeking.

Sheridan's plan for the Battle of Five Forks called for his 11,000 cavalry to attack the

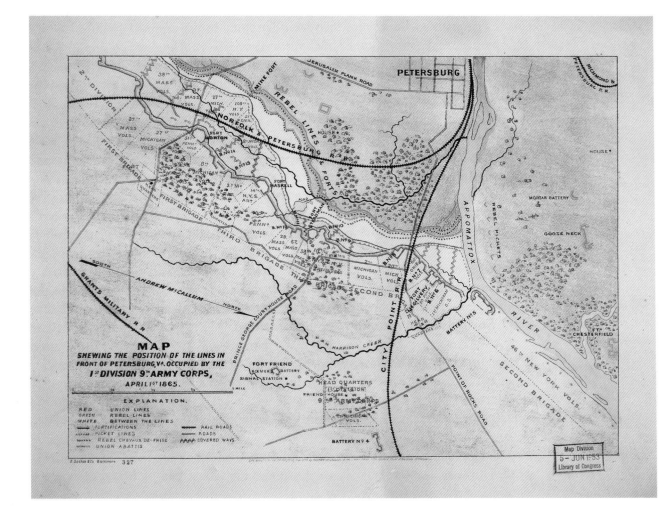

MAP
SHEWING THE POSITION OF THE LINES IN
FRONT OF PETERSBURG, VA. OCCUPIED BY THE
1ST DIVISION 9TH ARMY CORPS,
APRIL 1ST 1865.

EXPLANATION.

RED — UNION LINES
GREEN — REBEL LINES
WHITE — BETWEEN THE LINES
— FORTIFICATIONS
— PICKET LINES
— REBEL CHEVAUX DE-FRISE
— UNION ABATTIS
— RAIL ROADS
— ROADS
— COVERED WAYS

Confederates and pin them for a sweeping flank attack by Warren from the east. Because of confusing and delayed orders, Warren wasn't in place for the scheduled dawn attack, and Sheridan was furious. Around 4 p.m. the Fifth Corps moved out, only to discover that Pickett was entrenched farther west than thought. Maps of the area were terrible, and two of Warren's divisions attacked the empty White Oak Road, while a single division hit Pickett's flank by itself.

The hero of Little Round Top, Joshua Chamberlain, had recovered from terrible wounds in 1864 to lead one of the divisions marching into the woods. Chamberlain heard the fight off to his left, realized what had happened, and brought his force crashing down on the exposed Confederate flank. Warren rode on to bring the rest of his corps back into the battle.

Sheridan arrived as a Confederate counterattack threatened to drive Chamberlain off. Riding in front of his lines with his headquarters guidon, Sheridan personally led charge after charge, at one

The regimental frontage of each unit in the Union First Division, Ninth Corps is detailed in Nathaniel Michler's survey of the Petersburg lines as they appeared on April 1, 1865. At dawn the next morning, Grant launched an all-out assault that overran the Confederate defenses, and ended the nine-month siege.

point leaping his horse over the entrenchments to capture startled Rebel infantrymen.

Warren finally corralled his forces and brought them in behind Pickett's small army, nearly surrounding the Confederates and giving Sheridan one of the most complete victories of the war. Sheridan's cavalry under Custer and Merritt charged in from south and west, while Mackenzie came in from the east. More than 5,000 Rebels were captured, and the Rebels' morale was shattered. Pickett himself missed almost the entire battle; he was off eating shad caught by his cavalry commander, Tom Rosser, and some atmospheric freak prevented noise of the fight from reaching them.

Another casualty of the fight was Warren, who rode up in triumph to report the success of his attack only to have Sheridan remove him from command for lacking aggressiveness early in the fight. The capable Charles Griffin took over the Fifth Corps, and Warren spent the rest of his life seeking exoneration.

Grant immediately ordered the Sixth and Ninth Corps to attack along their front at Petersburg the next morning, Sunday, April 2. It would be over in days. But fights for Fort Gregg and control of the Rebel lines were fierce, as the Confederates realized that their choices had narrowed to death or surrender. Slowly at first, then as in the breaking of a dam the Federals swept across the lines which had defied them for nearly a year.

Charles W. Reed's sketch shows an awe-stricken soldier about to shake hands with Lincoln.

Lee was ill in bed, probably from rheumatism, when A.P. Hill and Longstreet, "Old Pete" barely recovered from his Wilderness wounds, arrived to report on the Federal attack. As they talked, it became the final breakthrough. Hill rode off to try and stabilize the lines long enough for Lee to retreat with the army through Richmond, and then out toward Appomattox. Lee had already told his commanders if it came to a breakout, try to rally at Amelia Court House, thirty-five miles west of Petersburg on the Richmond & Danville Railroad. Food and ammunition would be waiting.

As Hill approached his lines he was shot dead by advancing Union skirmishers. An aide returned to tell Lee, who quietly wept and said "He is at rest now, and we who are left are the ones to suffer." Lee telegraphed Secretary of War Breckenridge that Richmond must be abandoned. Word went to President Davis in church that it was over, it was time to go.

At dusk it became Walpurgis Night in Richmond as released felons, prostitutes, and deserters roamed the streets looting and drinking from broken liquor stores.

The heart of the Confederacy burned as its government and army fled into the night. The next day Richmond was occupied by black troops of the Twenty-fifth Corps.

Lincoln was at City Point when the collapse started, and he arrived in Richmond with his son Tad and walked the streets without an escort, a hero to the newly freed slaves. Witnesses said that Lincoln, though obviously happy, looked tired and worn down. Later he visited the Confederate White House and sat at Davis's desk.

Lee and his army were now fleeing southwest, divided into five separate forces, all hoping for food at Amelia Court House. But when Lee pulled in with the van of the army he was stunned to find that his exhausted staff, in the hasty retreat, hadn't made it clear that food was to be there. It was a crushing blow to troops already near defeat.

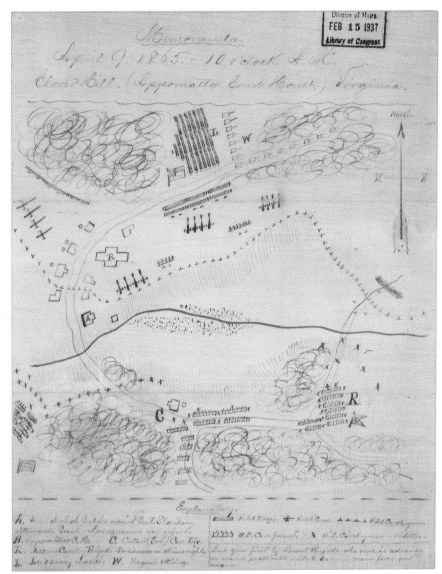

A crude pen-and-ink sketch by an anonymous Yankee soldier shows the situation at Appomattox Court House at 10 am of April 9, 1865. Later that day, his troops encircled and with no hope for a breakout, Robert E. Lee surrendered to Grant at the McLean House, marked "A" on the map.

Lee's retreat degenerated into a desperate search for food, and the Army of Northern Virginia was stretched longer and longer, making it increasingly vulnerable to Grant's infantry and cavalry units snapping on its flanks and heels.

The last great fight of the army, at Sayler's Creek on April 6, was the worst defeat ever suffered by Lee's men. The high command was by this point so exhausted they could barely move, much less issue coherent orders or remember to keep each other informed of changes in route and objective. The diminished corps of Dick Ewell and Richard Anderson were caught between the Union Sixth Corps and Sheridan's cavalry under Merritt.

The two Confederate forces battled back to back, separated by less than a mile. The fighting was as intense as any in the war, and some Rebel units actually broke the center of the Sixth Corps line. But the Federals overwhelmed the flanks of Ewell's men, while Custer, Devin, and Crook rode their cavalry over Anderson's lines to the south. One third of the Army of Northern Virginia was captured, between 7,000 and 8,000 men along with six generals, including Ewell, Joseph Kershaw, and Lee's son Custis.

A few thousand survivors straggled to rejoin Gordon and Longstreet, still trying to head west. Lee watched the aftermath in Sayler's Creek Valley from a hilltop, and cried "My God! Has the army dissolved?" General William Mahone tried to reassure his stricken commander, "No, General, here are troops ready to do their duty." But both men knew it was almost done.

That night, a triumphant Sheridan reported to Grant "If the thing is pressed I think Lee will surrender." Grant sent the message to Lincoln, still at City Point, who shot back "Let the thing be pressed." The night of April 7 Sheridan reported that Lee's provisions were waiting at Appomattox Station, twenty-six miles down the road, and that he was racing to capture them. Grant sat down and wrote Lee suggesting that the time had come to surrender: "The results of the past week must convince you of the hopelessness of further resistance."

Grant's offer reached Lee within hours; he handed the message to Longstreet, who said simply, "Not yet." Lee sent word to Grant that while he didn't think the time had arrived for the army to give up, he wanted to know "what terms you will offer on condition of its surrender" Without waiting for a response, Lee pulled his remaining forces quickly away towards Appomattox Court House.

The next day, a reply came hinting at the generous terms Lincoln had suggested in March at the conference with Grant and Sherman. Lee was surprised, and clearly relieved, and began to think that it might be time after all. But he resolved to try one more fight, one last attempt to break free. John B. Gordon, supported by Fitz Lee's cavalry, would try to clear the way through Custer's cavalry, known to be blocking the road to Lynchburg. If there was no Union infantry in support, it might work. Lee sent Grant another message stalling for time.

Sheridan again saw what was happening, and urged the Twenty-fourth Corps of E.O.C. Ord to march, march until they collapsed if necessary to win the race to Appomattox. Ord's men responded by covering thirty miles in twenty-one hours. When Gordon's men came up they brushed aside the Union cavalry screen to confront the Army of the James coming into line.

Longstreet, to the north of town, wheeled to find the Sixth Corps deploying against him. Lee had perhaps 23,000 soldiers; it was over. He said "Now there is nothing left me but to go see General Grant, and I had rather die a thousand deaths."

That night Robert E. Lee performed his greatest service to the country when he refused suggestions that the army disband and turn to guerrilla warfare. The next morning, April 9, he surrendered the Army of Northern Virginia to U.S. Grant.

———✦———

As at Chattanooga, the static situation around Petersburg allowed the Union to exploit its resources for good mapping operations and allowed the engineers time to spend laying out fortifications (p.162).

And also as at Chattanooga, the time for mapping proved of greatest value to the artillery. Major Nathaniel Michler (author of maps on pp. 79 and 169) reported:

"On learning the plan [that would become the Battle of the Crater] adopted I directed my principal assistant, Major John E. Weyss, to commence on the 9th an exact triangulation of the front of Petersburg, locating our own line of work as well as that of the enemy....

"By this triangulation, performed under the fire of the enemy's batteries and sharpshooters, the different spires and prominent buildings in Petersburg were located, and having been furnished by Professor Bache, Superintendent of the United States Coastal Survey, with a copy of the beautiful map of that city and the Appomattox River prepared a few years ago in his department, I was able to combine the two, and thereby obtain an exact and connected map of the locality of our siege operations, covering the whole ground occupied by both armies."

Major Michler's final report in March of 1865 is very similar:

"In the topographical department the triangulation parties are pushing forward the surveys between Fort Siebart and Hatcher's Run, and in the office, campaign maps are being prepared."

Sheridan's decisive victory at the Battle of Five Forks on April 1 (pp. 169-170), doomed the last Confederate railroad into Petersburg, the Norfolk and Petersburg (also known as the Southside) Railroad (shown on the Michler map, p. 169). The next day, Grant ordered a general assault on the lines that shattered the thinly stretched gray line and began the race that would end at Appomattox.

Appomattox became an overnight tourist attraction. After four years of long and bloody war, the violence was finally at an end, and the jubilant Northern public wanted any mementos of Lee's surrender. Some of the earliest press included maps of the final dispositions, such as the view on page 160, and even sketches became collector's items (p. 171). The troop positions were not militarily important, because the issue was never in doubt, but anything relating to Appomattox represented a snapshot of history.

With the end of the fratricidal war that had cost 620,000 American lives, Grant's and Sherman's victorious blue-clad armies held a massive two-day victory parade down Washington's Pennsylvania Avenue. It was "an army of tested manhood," General Joshua Chamberlain declared, "clothed with power, crowned with glory, marching to its dissolution!" LC B811-3315

Aftermath

The maps which proved so important to the advancing armies proved equally valuable to the civilians after the war. In 1861, the young country was still a poorly charted wilderness, and the campaigns of an unexpected war often required information that was simply unavailable. Although growing population and commerce had resulted in improved topographical knowledge and better maps, it was ironically the scourge of war that left the greatest legacy of well-made maps in its wake.

Bibliography

Alexander, Edward P. *Fighting for the Confederacy.* Chapel Hill: University of North Carolina Press, 1989.

Andrews, Harris, et. al. *Photographs of American Civil War Cavalry.* East Stroudsburg, Pa: Guidon Press, 1988.

Boatner, Mark M. III. *The Civil War Dictionary.* New York: David McKay Co., 1959.

Burns, Ken, et. al. *The Civil War.* Alexandria, Va.: Time-Life Films, 9 vol. video, 1990.

Cooling, Benjamin F. Symbol, *Sword & Shield.* Hamden, Ct.: Archon, 1975.

Dana, William C. *Recollections of the Civil War.* New York: D. Appleton & Co., 1898.

Davis, William C. *The Battlefields of the Civil War.* New York: Smithmark Publishing, 1991.

Foley, Jack. *The Civil War.* Columbia, Md.: Classic Images, 10 vol. video, 1986-90.

Griffith, Paddy. *Battle Tactics of the Civil War.* New Haven: Yale University Press, 1987.

Holien, Kim B. *Battle at Ball's Bluff.* Orange, Va.: Moss Publications, 1985.

Keegan, John. *The Mask of Command.* New York: Viking Penguin, 1987.

Lewis, Thomas A. *The Guns of Cedar Creek.* New York: Harper & Row, 1988.

Liddell-Hart, B.H. *Sherman.* New York: Dodd, Mead & Co., 1929.

Linderman, Gerald F. *Embattled Courage.* New York: The Free Press, 1987.

Longacre, Edward G. *The Cavalry at Gettysburg.* Cranbury, NJ: Fairleigh Dickenson University Press, 1986.

McFeely, William. *Grant.* New York: W.H. Norton & Co., 1981.

Pohanka, Brian & Abell, Sam. *The Civil War: An Aerial Portrait.* Charlottesville, Va.: Thomasson-Grant, 1990.

Schurz, Carl. *The Reminiscences of Gen. Carl Schurz.* New York: The McClure Co., 1907.

Sears, Stephen W. *Landscape Turned Red.* New Haven: Ticknor & Fields, 1983.

Sherman, William T. *Memoirs.* New York: Charles Webster & Co., 1892.

Smith, Page. *Trial by Fire.* New York: McGraw Hill, 1982.

Sommers, Richard J. *Richmond Redeemed.* New York: Doubleday & Co., 1981.

Starr, Stephen Z. *The Union Cavalry in the Civil War.* Baton Rouge: LSU Press, 1979.

Stephenson, Richard W. *Civil War Maps.* Washington, DC: The Library of Congress, 1989.

Symonds, Craig L. A. *Battlefield Atlas.* Baltimore: The Nautical and Aviation Publishing Company of America, 1983.

Time-Life Books. *The Civil War.* 27 vols. Alexandria, Va. 1983-87.

Trudeau, Noah A. *Bloody Roads South.* Boston: Little Brown, 1989.

Wert, Jeffery D. *Mosby's Rangers.* New York: Simon & Schuster, 1990.

Wilson, Edmund. *Patriotic Gore.* New York: Random House, 1962.

INDEX